"Many years ago, Dr. J.I. Packer compiled a list of books that he commended to his readers. He labelled his five-star top quality books those books 'you must sell your shirt to purchase.' This book on the true nature of saving faith I would unhesitatingly put into that category. It is lucid, fresh, brief, scholarly, readable, relevant, heart-warming, humbling and suitable for the novice Christian as well as someone who has known the Lord Jesus Christ for decades. Everyone who reads it, wishing to know what is the true understanding of a faith that is the means of our salvation, will find much assistance to their walk with God in these pages."

Geoffrey Thomas
Visiting professor of Historical Theology,
Puritan Reformed Theological Seminary.

"Christianity has seen more than its share of debates and controversies. Some of them are little more than tempests in a teacup. Some of them are clearly important, but over what we might call 'secondary issues,' where there is legitimate disagreement and fellowship in the Gospel sis till possible. But some of them have dealt with absolutely primary matters, where affirmations or denials bear eternal consequence. The subject of this well-written, well-argued book falls clearly into the latter category: what does the Bible mean by saving faith? In other words, what does the Bible teach about how a person is saved from eternal wrath and hell? In a nutshell, Dr. Osterbrock provides the reader with a succinct and perspicuous summary of what the Bible teaches on this vital subject. All in all, an informative read bespangled with sparkling prose and spiritual refreshment!"

Michael A.G. Haykin
Chair and professor of church history,
The Southern Baptist Theological Seminary.

"In *What Is Saving Faith?* Christopher Ellis Osterbrock explores the biblical and essential Christian doctrine, faith. I welcome this well-written book on saving faith for its theological underpinning and its practical application. Definitions are important but Osterbrock is not content with definitions *alone*. He offers explanation *and* he provides guidance as to how to live by faith. This book will help you to understand faith as God's gift that is to be employed for his glory in accordance with his Word. I heartily commend this work for your consideration."

Ray Rhodes, Jr.
Author, *Susie: The Life and Legacy of Susannah Spurgeon* and *Yours, till Heaven, the untold Love Story of Charles and Susie Spurgeon.*

"Grounded in Scripture, guarded by the confessions, and guided by a myriad of theologians, *What Is Saving Faith?* successfully answers that question—and in a way that is wonderfully accessible to those asking it. Christopher Osterbrock's definition of saving faith as an 'affectionate knowledge' is worthy of use not only by pastors instructing their congregations, but also by parents instructing their children."

Josh Niemi
Founder, Expository Parenting Ministries

"*What Is Saving Faith?* is a great short introduction to the various aspects of faith. What I love about it most is its seamless weaving of thoughts on faith from various great thinkers in the Christian tradition. You'll be introduced to everyone from John Owen to Charles Hodge to Andrew Fuller to Herman Bavinck. It's hard to find a book that doesn't shy away from these great thinkers and yet is designed for church members. It's written in an informal conversational style that lay readers will enjoy and rests upon the historic Reformed confessions in its exposition. It's well worth your time."

Jordan L. Steffaniak
Co-Founder, The London Lyceum;
Research Fellow, The Center for Faith and Culture at Southeastern Seminary

What Is Saving Faith?

WHAT IS SAVING FAITH?

CHRISTOPHER ELLIS OSTERBROCK

What Is Saving Faith?
Copyright © Christopher Ellis Osterbrock 2022

All rights reserved. This book or any portion thereof may not be reproduced or used in any manner whatsoever without the express written permission of the publisher except for the use of brief quotations in a book review.

Published by: H&E Publishing, Peterborough, Ontario
www.hesedandemet.com

Paperback ISBN: 978-1-77484-044-3
Ebook ISBN: 978-1-77484-045-0

The Gifted Tether

His rope the hand is gripping fast
 And pulling without strain
Fingers trust not sail and mast
 And loosen not for pain
Where heart finds warmth or frigid wind
 The mind on deck is sure
Christ's ferry proves the journey's end
 The Word–His rope–secure

Pilgrim, fasten to the gift in hand
Know it's anchored to His promised land
Forfeit the sails, they catch worldly dross
By rope alone we're pulled to the Cross

~ ~ ~

To Rev. Dr. David B. Smith
A Pastor. A Brother. A Friend

Contents

Foreword i
    Nate Pickowicz
Preface 1

1. How do we define saving faith? 5
2. How do we receive faith? 15
3. Can we be assured of our faith? 27
4. How do we defend against false faith? 39
5. How can I practice my faith? 55
6. If faith is a gift, then why evangelize? 71
Conclusion 87

Excursus:
On *saving faith* and the biblical language of amounts 91
Selected bibliography 99
Acknowledgments 107
Index 109
Scripture Index 113

Foreword

Over the last few decades, we have seen the emergence of the "megachurch"—thousands of people crammed into large church buildings for Sunday services. Admittedly, these events are often geared toward "seekers" who are interested in knowing more about Jesus Christ, which, on the surface, appears to be a wonderful thing. Every year these churches report massive numbers of conversions; professions of faith made by these church attendees. When the numbers are evaluated, however, a very different picture begins to emerge.

Several studies have found that, of the large numbers of professions obtained in many of the megachurch church events, a disappointingly small number of them have manifested a spiritual commitment in the months and years to follow. In his 2015 book, *The Prodigal Church*, Jared C. Wilson cites several of these studies, including the now-famous REVEAL study conducted at Willow Creek Community Church in Chicago. Despite explosive numerical growth, only a small number of churchgoers reported to be growing in their Christian faith, with several more disenfranchised with the church altogether. In his evaluation, Wilson concluded that "one can have the appearance of success and yet not actually be succeeding."[1] What is the reason for such false and superficial Christianity? While Wilson offers his own postulations, it is not hard to see

---

[1] Jared C. Wilson, *The Prodigal Church: A Gentle Manifesto against the Status Quo* (Wheaton, IL: Crossway, 2015), 39.

that a fundamental problem is a lack of a true work of God in many of the people who profess faith in Jesus Christ.

At the core of the problem is the pervasiveness of false faith, or *easy-believism*. The general idea behind this is that, if you can persuade a person make a profession of faith, it will be sufficient to save them and turn them into a Christian. Of course, careful evaluation of any ministry or movement is needed, but it is very often a wrong view of salvation and regeneration that leads to manipulative tactics in the hope of producing mass conversions. However, this error is not new to our current era. Much of our modern American evangelistic methodology comes to us from nineteenth-century century preacher, Charles G. Finney.

Finney often hailed as one of the heroes of the Second Great Awakening. No doubt a brilliant, earnest, and influential man, Finney engaged in large-scale "revivals" that boasted a wave of new converts to Christianity. The key component to Finney's crusades was the use of "new measures" to generate conversions. Finney famously noted that he did not believe revival to be a divine miracle, as was held by the majority of church history. Rather, he stated that "a revival is the result of the *right* use of the appropriate means."[2] In other words, a gospel minister could employ the right tactics at the right time in the right way and effectually produce a genuine response from the would-be believer.

While his methods flew in the face of historic Christianity, Finney was convinced of the correctness of his own theology and practice. According to Iain Murray, Finney appealed to both his own personal experience of success in ministry, as well

---

[2] Charles G. Finney, *Revival Lectures* (Old Tappan, NJ: The Fleming H. Revell Company, 1868), 5.

FOREWORD

as the perceived barrenness of the prevailing orthodoxy, which he deemed to be "hyper-Calvinism."[3] In short, he did what he did because it *worked*—at least superficially. People came out in droves to hear his sermons and, like clockwork, responded with emotional professions of faith. However, Scripture teaches that genuine conversion is not a work of human invention or effort, but an inner work of the heart accomplished by the Holy Spirit, whereby a person hears and understands the gospel, and responds by faith in Jesus Christ (John 3:3-8; Rom. 10:17; etc.).

Many in modern Christianity have employed the same pragmatic tactics of Charles Finney in their own ministries, but this pragmatism has not produced the desired results. In fact, "pragmatism," writes Wilson, "is killing the spiritual life of congregations, even congregations seeing an increase in attendance to Sunday worship."[4] All of the effort and energy to manufacture spiritual life within the church is useless unless we understand how a person becomes a Christian and lives in obedience to Christ—*by faith*. And not just a quick, easy profession of generic faith, but a genuine, informed, Spirit-wrought saving faith in the person and work of Jesus Christ.

It is easy to critique large movements and make sweeping generalizations, but when we peel back the layers, we are left to address those *individuals* who are caught up in the fray. After all, these are human souls whose eternity hangs in the balance. We cannot afford to play games and misconstrue or misunderstand how a person obtains salvation in Jesus Christ.

---

[3] Iain H. Murray, *Pentecost—Today?* (Edinburgh: The Banner of Truth Trust, 1998), 43-46.

[4] Wilson, *The Prodigal Church*, 148.

What is Saving Faith?

In the end, we are faced with several key questions, namely: *What is saving faith? How do you lay hold of it? What does it mean to have faith?* Thankfully, Christopher Osterbrock addresses these questions and more in the following pages. Not only does he give us biblical, theological, and historical content, he also labors to explain and evaluate it. His concern is palpable. He really cares that you understand the nature of your faith in Jesus Christ, as well as how to minister the gospel for the benefit of the faith of others.

May the Lord use this book as a fine crafting tool to chisel away error and polish the fine edges of sound doctrine.

Soli Deo gloria!

Nate Pickowicz
November 2021
Gilmanton Iron Works, N.H.

Preface

"I don't *feel* any different," I remember explaining to a close friend shortly after my baptism. I wondered, should I be acting a certain way now so people can see that I'm saved? Should I act overjoyed, weepy, emotional? This question must be on the minds of so many who go through baptism without a clear understanding of faith. I've never been the type of person to act outwardly one way or another (I'm far too often stuck in my own head). That afternoon, I waited for a response to my confession of stoicism. The response came to me about a dozen years later, through my study of the Puritans. Faith doesn't require warm, fuzzy feelings. Neither does it require attaining to a certain degree of knowledge. Rather, saving faith requires the work of the Holy Spirit enlivening the heart and renewing the mind. I can't perform *any* kind of work to develop that new life on my own—I'm dead in sin. I believe I was changed prior to my baptism; I was regenerated by the Holy Spirit and through him I desired to know more and more about the present work of Jesus Christ and the mystery of his union within me. The Spirit gifted me an affectionate knowledge. As I look back on that day, I realize eighteen-year-old Christopher was experiencing saving faith—no matter how I *felt* about it. So, the question remains: how does faith work?

This book is designed to help you explore the typical questions that arise from thinking through the teachings on faith. It is an essential to the Christian life; therefore, we ought to show diligence as we seek to know what the Bible says. The Lord blesses those who seek the deep things of doctrine (Heb. 11:6), so as you explore the essentials with me, my prayer is for you to grow in grace and truth.

The doctrine of saving faith is an historically rich doctrine that doesn't seem to come up on its own too often. We typically reserve the subject of faith for the equally necessary doctrine of justification by faith. When saving faith does come up, professional theologians naturally use terms like *notitia* (notion or knowledge), *assensus* (assent), and *fiducia* (fidelity or trust). While these words are essential in the scholarship of the subject, they're not particularly helpful to those like my younger self who desired to know how I use the gift God has given me to believe. We need a proper understanding as to what exactly we are trying to communicate. These ideas will certainly be found throughout the chapters below, but the approach will be a bit different. The goal of this small volume is to explore this essential doctrine with questions many Christians really might like to ask. For this reason, and because I have personally found the study enriching to my spiritual life and evangelism, I present to you a concise study on our doctrine. This is meant for your spiritual edification, to clarify what the term *saving faith* means and how the affections it produces benefit your personal walk. Let's not meet this word *faith* in abstract, loosely defined ways. If we are to grow in our faith, then we must know the meaning of the term! Let's sit down and spend some time thinking through this provocative, deep, and nourishing doctrine together.

Outline of our study

Chapter 1 is designed to help us think through a definition of the term saving faith that brings together the objective truth of

Preface

the things we believe and the spiritual experience of living out that truth.

Chapter 2 discusses how the supernatural gift of faith is received by humans and how we experience new life when faith shows up.

Chapter 3 leads us to understand the ramifications of this supernatural gift; if it cannot be lost, then how can I be assured I am saved all the time?

Chapter 4 asks what are the consequences of counterfeit faiths that might show up within the church? We examine how to defend the biblical understanding of saving faith by learning what to watch for in our spiritual lives.

Chapter 5 teaches how to grow and exercise our faith through right spiritual practices, growing even beyond obedience and repentance.

Chapter 6 addresses the spiritual practice and command of evangelism, for though saving faith is a gift of God, believers are compelled by God to be an evangelizing people.

A conclusion gives a final note of encouragement as you study this rich biblical doctrine of saving faith.

As this resource is meant for the church's edification, each chapter ends with several questions designed to be asked within a small group setting or for personal meditation—to strengthen your faith!

So then, let's ask this question with heartfelt desire for God's glory, what is *saving faith*?

1
How do we define saving faith?

Two men were boarding a plane. The first man was called to the gate, received his boarding pass, and proceeded down the aisle to his window seat, where he was safely fastened. As he peaked out of his window, he observed an interesting sight out on the airstrip. The second man threw himself over a fence, raced down the tarmac, and proceeded to climb onto the wing of the plane, gripping hold of the curved metal with all his might. Both men were ready to fly, but which of them evidence a *saving* faith?

Misunderstanding the term *faith*
I don't know about you, but there are plenty of times I've ended up on the wing, passionately gripping on to some particular song or experience as the crux of my faith. In ministry, I've sought to conjure some feeling for the sake of manipulating an emotional response out of my hearers. But faith, according to New Testament wording, refers to belief or believing. Those who are described as faithful, are described as "believing ones" (see the Greek text of the *whosoever*s in John 3:16–18). They evidence a particular relationship with the thing or rather the person believed—he is our object of faith, not the expressions or experiences resulting from his presence.

Our inability to define our faith is rooted in our *preference* for how we believe, rather than the *object* on whom we believe. We use texts to prove an objective truth in math, science, or history, but too often rely on emotions-based experiences to get others to believe in Christ (or even to assure ourselves of *our* belief in Christ). Emotions are a gift from God, a true and useful blessing, but they are consequences of, or tools for, growing in faith. We get it in our heads that evangelism, or even personal growth, is a method wherein we must use manipulation to repeat some memorable experience. What we're really doing is "believing" in a subjective feeling. Faith, then, however consciously, is dependent upon exertions, flying in the face of Romans 9:16. Faith ought to be rooted in the nutrient-rich soil of God's word (Luke 8:15).

As we approach the term through this study, my concern is for you to see faith as a gift from God where you are, at once, made to know and grow in the certain truths of our object of faith. Even on the night of Christ's birth the shepherds had the gospel "made known" to them out of nowhere, while they were living in darkness, without earning, working, or experiencing any feeling but fear of God's glory (Luke 2:15). Saving faith joins together the act of salvation and the living experiment of Christian life—*both* are given and understood through Scripture (1 Pet. 1:22–23). Let's go there now.

Faith and propositions

What does the Bible say concerning faith? The Bible is clear that it alone holds the truths necessary for salvation (2 Tim. 3:15). Likewise, it teaches certain truths upon which we are called to affirm, hope, submit, obey, desire—and all of these are held in the object of our faith, Jesus Christ. Jesus is keeping no secret when he says, "believe what is said about me" (John 8:24). We believe because of his grace to make us do so. Grace is the means to obtain faith, and faith is the means to know who

How do we define saving faith?

has redeemed us by such sovereign grace.[1] Faith is directly connected to knowledge; and not just any knowledge, but an assured, lived-out knowledge of who Christ is and what he does (Heb. 11:1-3). These bits of knowledge from Scripture's authority are what we might call faith statements: concrete, salient points, theologians have referred to as propositions. An example of a pro-position is, "Jesus Christ was born of a virgin." This is a truth about our object of faith, about theology. We are called to grow in the multitude of propositions we learn from Scripture, to meditate on how they join together and how we apply them to our practice, a right expression of faith.

Generations of men and women have faithfully placed, pursued, and grown their faith upon Jesus Christ using such eternal propositions. Truly, the divine object is eternal, so that which is spoken of him ought to be regarded as eternally true and faithful. We are not only called to believe on, but to live in the truths we find in Scripture. We may affirm God's gift of special revelation, but without saving faith, we do not cling to or trust the person of Christ revealed in Scripture. Our hearts, through faith, are only satisfied in the *right* object of our faith, or as Andrew Fuller says, "Our hearts must be as Christ's heart, or we are not one with him."[2] His divine revelation shapes our reality, a new reality of our union in Jesus Christ.

Faith is not only affirming or agreeing with the propositions of Scripture, but affection toward the one of whom Scripture speaks. Affection is a term used to express our desires,

---

[1] John Murray, *The Epistle to the Romans*, NICNT (Grand Rapids, MI: Wm. B. Eerdmans, 1968), 27 fn21. Murray does not exaggerate the wonderful power of this gift when he notes "Wherever there is faith, there the omnipotence of God is operative unto salvation. This is a law with no exceptions" (28). Think of what that means for the intimate power of our received relationship.

[2] Andrew Fuller, *Strictures on Sandemanianism in Twelve Letters to a Friend* (New York: Richard Scott, 1812), 152.

motivations, the very appetite of our hearts. Faith is more than cognitive knowledge. Scripture's propositions lead us to a particular intimacy with God; not just that we know the things of God, but that we grow in relationship with him by such knowledge. Such knowledge brings us to align ourselves with his will and affections, as well as to right worship. K. Scott Oliphint describes knowledge as not just facts, but a passionate compulsion to be with a person. He writes, "Theology is to be God-centered; it comes from him, it should teach us more and more about him, and that teaching should lead us inexorably to praise him. Does our theology do that?"[3]

Propositions enliven within us a new reality wherein we live and grow with the Holy Spirit. Saving faith is the exercise of this new way of living, a way where truth isn't just an abstraction, but an affection that gives our lives a new and eternal purpose. So, how can we cultivate a definition that embraces the objective propositions of Scripture *and* the personal affections we are to experience?

Cultivating our definition
Nowhere but in our Bible is faith seen as the freely gifted intimate relationship found in Jesus Christ. Such intense intimacy with the Divine in the Christian life is something no other religion understands. Intimacy of faith is most poignantly shown through Ephesians 2:8-9: "For by grace you have been saved through faith. And this is not your own doing; it is the gift of God, not a result of works, so that no one may boast" (See also Eph. 1:15-18ff).

---

[3] K. Scott Olihpint, *The Majesty of Mystery: Celebrating the Glory of an Incomprehensible God* (Bellingham, WA: Lexham Press, 2016), 21.

How do we define saving faith?

The majority of church fathers held faith as the "gift" of Ephesians 2:8. At the very least, grace *and* faith are put together under the "gift" language. This use of the term suggests faith as the means or mechanism for receiving God's grace.[4] Every attempt to say we have believed enough or had our own special experience that saved us is boastful arrogance. We desire personal affection, craving the experience and intimacy that we recognize in Christ. However, such affections only come through the means Christ gives. Do not chase the feeling; chase the Word. Trust the Giver to give the gift rightly, and within his sovereign plan. The gift of faith is more than a means for receiving grace, it is the very hand of Christ (John 10:28) tarrying with us through this life, that we might grow in and conform to the righteousness of God.

A gift such as this deserves a special definition; here is what we will work with through this study:

> Saving faith is a gift of God, whereby the Holy Spirit enlivens us to know, desire, and live according to the biblical doctrines of Jesus Christ. He draws us to be inclined to trust and experience Jesus more, especially in sharing the truths of his Word. In the simplest terms, saving faith is affectionate knowledge of the scriptural truths of the person and object of our faith: Jesus Christ.

---

[4] Matthew Olliffe, *Is 'Faith' the 'Gift of God'? Reading Ephesians 2:8-10 with the Ancients* (https://au.thegospelcoalition.org/article/is-faith-the-gift-of-god-reading-ephesians-28-10-with-the-ancients). Matthew Olliffe points out succinctly seven of the church fathers; Chrysostom, Jerome, Augustine, Theodoret, Fulgentius, Oecumenius, and Theophylact. Olliffe likewise shows how many of these early Greek theologians struggled with this verse because they knew the appropriate exegesis but held to faith as a solely human work. For the construction of this verse, see Benjamin L. Merkle, *Ephesians*, Exegetical Guide to the Greek New Testament (Nashville, TN: B&H, 2016), 61.

WHAT IS SAVING FAITH?

The *1689 Baptist Confession of Faith* expresses saving faith as, "The grace of faith, whereby the elect are enabled to believe to the saving of their souls, [it] is the work of the Spirit of Christ in their hearts, and is ordinarily [worked] by the ministry of the Word; by which also it is increased and strengthened."[5]

God expresses his intimacy to those he loves by enabling them to know and trust what he says of himself. Feelings are always subordinate to his gift. Our understanding of the power in faith is faulty, but the Spirit changes us. Francis Turretin comments that saving faith, in its certainty and truth, "is not human or fallible, but divine and infallible."[6] Faith, a work absent from us until regeneration, is what Christ uses to raise us up in the power of God (Col. 2:12). Emotions, feelings, psychological manifestations, and the expression of divine presence fluctuate throughout the believer's life until New Eden (at best these are subordinate means to draw us to Scripture, at worst the devices of Satan to lead us away from the truths of Christ). When we subordinate our subjective responses, then we are ordering them properly and using them as in submission to the Lord—in such a way even those strange experiences can be a means to grow in the experience of God's grace.

All of us are fallible, given to doubt, to feel as though we're far from God, or that the Lord is silent. We're prone to overthink how frequently we wax and wane in the spiritual life. Our natural inclinations may even trust the deceiver's tongue, which tells us that we must have another experience to really be sure we're saved. But the gospel gets it right. Your faith is

---

[5] *The 1689 Baptist Confession of Faith in Modern English* (Cape Coral, FL: Founders, 2012, 2017), 32. See chapter 14.1. Also included for strengthening and increasing faith are the ordinances of baptism and the Lord's Supper as well as prayer.

[6] Francis Turretin, *Institutes of Elenctic Theology*, ed. James T. Dennison, Jr., trans. George Musgrave Giger (Phillipsburg, NJ: P&R, 1994), 2:617.

perfectly gifted, not controlled by your exertions or will (John 1:13), nor is it grown into salvation, but chiefly given simultaneously in salvation for the purpose of progressing in holiness.

Through Scripture propositions, and doctrine built thereon, the Spirit is nourishing the believer with life-giving words, even through our wanderings in the wilderness of this earthly life, even for the sake of our journeying through trial and temptation. It is not our position to ensure our faith; if we are Bible-believers, then we recognize Jesus Christ as the author and finisher of our faith.

Distinctively *saving* faith
Going forward, why are we to use the descriptor *saving*? We use this descriptor for a minimum of three reasons: first, *saving* is passive in the sense that receiving the gift of faith comes solely by the work of regeneration, faith is a gift that does not come from the recipient (John 6:63-65; 1 John 5:1). Second, *saving* faith implies that the recipient is saved both *from* and *to* something. Faith saves us *from* the wrath of God, the depravity of our conscience and our sinful desires (Rom. 5:9; 12:2). Faith saves us *to* a life of obedience and affections toward our precious Christ (Col. 3:17). Third, *saving* denotes that this is a new and permanent station (John 6:39, 44; 18:9; 1 Cor. 1:8-9). If it does not come from us and it is the manner by which the Spirit involves us in regeneration, then it cannot be overcome by us. We are saved by faith and we will see our salvation bear fruit, not just in our present but in our eternal future (Job 42:2; Eph. 1:4-6). Only a *saving* faith generates permanency.

Quality over quantity

The Christian-doubter's question: how do I know if I'm on the wing or in the seat? The answer: by affectionate knowledge of propositions—not that you love the knowledge for itself, but you desire for intimacy with the one such knowledge reveals. One scene that illustrates our distinction is the three men on the cross. King Jesus hangs as the object of our faith. On either side are two men rightly condemned and crucified (Luke 23:33). One spends his dying breaths mocking Jesus (Luke 23:39), believing full well that Jesus exists and has performed miracles, perhaps even entertained by such miracles. The second, knowing little more than the other, rebukes the first and calls out to Jesus as his only savior (Luke 23:40-43). The second man was not saved by the quantity of his knowledge, but by the one who brought out affections for such knowledge—quality, not quantity.

Knowledge alone did not save the thief on the cross (and his personal experience was certainly nothing to boast of), but without the right kind of knowledge he'd never enter paradise. And if he relied on personal experience, he'd find nothing but despair. He looked to Jesus and believed with certainty on the object of his faith. The other, unsaved thief knew enough about Jesus—may even have agreed with some of the realities about Jesus—but his knowledge was wasted; it did not lead to affections. Such affectionate knowledge comes only by the gifting of the Holy Spirit.

Spiritual growth is always occasioned by intellectual and practical growth in Scripture by what we've called propositions. Yes, God's providence orchestrates personal experiences for our growth *in* the propositions of Scripture. Yet, when mystical encounters and miraculous experiences occur in

Scripture, they are occasioned to affirm a truth of doctrine. To divorce faith from knowledge would be to grab hold of the wing and seek after the exhilarating emotions of take-off ... and then fall headlong into our own subjective aether. Grounding ourselves in this doctrine will assure that we're secure, even against all turbulent winds.

Conclusion
As we proceed through this study, be assured that we are not hanging on the wing of blind zeal, but firmly planted in the seat and fastened to a biblical doctrine of *saving* faith. The goal of defining faith is a better grasp on sanctification, obedience, assurance, and a number of other doctrines. Assurance of our standing with God is impossible until we are certain we are standing by faith alone. "Through him we have also obtained access by faith into this grace in which we stand, and we rejoice in hope of the glory of God" (Rom. 5:2). Let's marvel together at how we receive this supernatural faith in the next chapter.

Examining our affections:

1. How do *you* define the word faith? What might the descriptor *saving* contribute to a definition?
2. How has your concept of faith changed or evolved since you first received Christ?
3. Describe an experience that led you to affirm a scriptural proposition like our example above, or perhaps one that leads to certain truths of God's attributes and character? How might your faith grow differently if you trust experiences rather than propositions such as these?
4. In what ways are the terms faith and salvation distinct? In what ways are they related?
5. What are the means we commonly use to grow in our faith? What do you imagine would be the next steps of discipleship for the thief on the cross, had he not been on the cross?
6. How might you explain *saving* faith to someone outside of the church? How might a discussion about affectionate knowledge change the atmosphere of an evangelistic encounter in comparing such a dialogue with one of convincing a person of a generic higher power?

2
How do we receive faith?

I'm terrible at gifts—not only in giving them, but in remembering who gave them to me a year later. Have you ever cleaned out a desk drawer and wondered, where on earth did this come from? When it comes to faith, I want to remember it the same way as the thief on the cross, who knew the source of his gift and received it with certainty, fully and completely. We receive faith as an undeserved gift of God, by means of his scriptural revelation to us. This "Grand Deposit" is bestowed upon us that we might be made trustworthy stewards of the gospel account.[1] We were dead in sin, then enlivened by the Spirit, made to know the mysteries of God, empowered to purge our sinful habits, and grow in affectionate knowledge of Jesus—this is receiving faith. But, when Peter says we have obtained faith (2 Pet. 1:1), what does *obtaining* look like?

The dead come to life

The first great truth in Scripture is that we are spiritually dead. We need to be saved. Before the Holy Spirit enters us, our will is irreversibly broken and we are not free to please God—no one is righteous (Rom. 3:10-11), we are born in iniquity (Ps. 51:5), with hearts darkened in deceit (Jer. 17:7; Eph. 4:18). That is what spiritually dead means. A corpse cannot resuscitate itself: no amount of effort can change that—we need to be born

---

[1] Bruce A. Ware, *God's Greater Glory: The Exalted God of Scripture and the Christian Faith* (Wheaton, IL: Crossway, 2004), 211. Ware rightly points to 1 Timothy 6:20; 2 Timothy 1:14; and Jude 3 as evidence that faith is a deposit from God. As a deposit, we are stewards of those collected, innumerable propositions that lead to our assurance of steadfast hope.

again! Of ourselves we will never understand the spiritual truths of Scripture. No matter how hard we try to believe, our hearts, eyes, and ears are darkened and incapable of knowing the things of God with any affection (1 Cor. 2:3-15). By God's steadfast love for his elect, he makes those dead in sin come alive—by grace you have been saved. This is the way he has chosen to receive his own glory (Ezek. 36:22-36). We must realize how dead we are in order to comprehend the steadfast and miraculous love of God that makes sinners into saints. The Lord will move those whom he chose (Eph. 1:4) to be born again (Acts 13:48). Augustine of Hippo (354-430) once quipped, "Faith is granted unasked for."[2] When someone is born again (John 3:3) the theological term is *regeneration*. We cannot believe on Christ without the Spirit, as John Bunyan preached in his last sermon: "Believing is the consequence of new birth." Faith comes by regeneration; no one can boast because it is a gift wrought by the Holy Spirit permanently dwelling as the new light of understanding in our eyes (John 14:17, 26; Gal. 5:22, "faithfulness" is a gift).

Regeneration

An anecdote from Charles Hodge (1797-1878) describes saving faith poetically as "the first conscious exercise of the renewed soul."[3] Through the analogy of a blind man experiencing sight for the first time, Hodge shows how this man has no control over how his eyes now see; he is passive in this act. His "conscious exercise," his work or part in the equation, is the new ability to discern reality. God makes his people alive for the

---

[2] Augustine of Hippo, *On the Free Choice of the Will, On Grace and Free Choice, and Other Writings*, ed. Peter King (New York: Cambridge, 2010), 164.
[3] Charles Hodge, *Systematic Theology*, vol. 3 (Peabody, MA: Hendrickson, 2016), 41.

How do we receive faith?

sake of experiencing his Spirit alive in them. The effort is not in believing, though that's an implication of saving faith. The effort is *rightly* placing our affection in the object of our faith as we are exposed to the truths of God. We then spend our life opening the packaging and learning the inseparable nature of the Giver and his gift.

From the beginning of his ministry, evangelist George Whitefield (1714-1770) taught that "illumination of the mind and the implanting of faith in the heart are entirely the work of the Holy Spirit."[4] His understanding of regeneration was based in Christ's love for the elect. Our love for God's truth ("love the truth and be saved," 2 Thess. 2:10) is the saving power we receive from the Holy Spirit to first trust in his Word and then pursue it with conviction. Though we see the work of regeneration only after our receiving faith, let's be sure to clarify regeneration precedes faith. Faith was implanted to trust the things we believe, and we believe because our mind was renewed by the Spirit.

No person can experience saving faith apart from the Spirit's work in regenerating souls. The *1689 Baptist Confession of Faith* offers a wonderful exposition of this doctrine:

> He enlightens their minds spiritually and savingly to understand the things of God. He renews their wills and by His almighty power turns them to good and effectually draws them to Jesus Christ. This effectual call flows from God's free and special grace alone, not from anything at all foreseen in those called. Neither does the call arise from any power or action on their part; they

---

[4] Arnold Dallimore, *George Whitefield* (Carlisle, PA: Banner of Truth, 1996), 1:137. Evangelism is absolutely necessary for the new birth to actually happen, thus the lifelong ministry of the great evangelist.

are totally passive in it. They are dead in sins and trespasses until they are made alive and renewed by the Holy Spirit. By this they are enabled to answer this call and to embrace the grace offered and conveyed in it. This response is enabled by a power that is no less than that which raised Christ from the dead.

Some might be enamored by the Word of God and believe some of its propositions; even so, if they are not born again, they will not experience a true and saving faith, an affectionate knowledge. Such are those plants that spring up only to be devoured, scorched, or strangled by the affections of this world (Mark 4:3-9).

An "assent" of heart

Regeneration brings about saving faith, but then what happens? William Ames (1576-1633) articulates that faith is far more than assent to knowledge—at its core it is assent of the heart.[5] Our declaration of assent, our "I believe!" (or what we might call affirmation), flows out of God changing our will. By his will we are made to believe (Phil. 1:29). We live out a new reality where Christ is Lord over us and where we desire to honor him. As our Lord, he requires our obedience, but as our Savior he also brings us into obedience by his Spirit within us. We *want* to serve him with obedience, not just by changed behavior but by transformed affections. That is assent of the heart. Look to the picture painted for us in Abraham (Gen. 15:6). His faith was counted as righteousness, not because he was good, but because the Lord changed his heart (Rom. 4:3). Abraham experienced his faith by following the promises of God, whether or

---

[5] William Ames, *Marrow of Theology*, ed. John Dystra Eusden (Grand Rapids, MI: Baker, 1997), 159.

not they made perfect sense, whether he *felt* one way or another, even through mistakes and divine silence, he humbled himself and chose (by the power of the indwelling Spirit) to desire after the Lord.

In 1 Peter 1:23, assent is all about obtaining "through the living and abiding word of God." Scripture propositions are essential, but these statements are about a person, and our relationship with him. Abraham applied the truth of God and left all else to follow after the promise *and* the person. J. Gresham Machen wrote, "Assent to certain propositions is not the whole of faith, but it is an absolutely necessary element in faith."[6] We affirm the truths of Scripture, and bear their fruit through our heads, hearts, and hands. All Scripture is assented to even if not all Scripture is known or understood, because our inclinations have been utterly changed to *want* to assent, to grow in an otherworldly intimacy with the Word made flesh (John 1:14), the object of faith.

Knowing not gnostic
We have not changed much since the first century church. We are a people who like finding new mechanisms or things to do, flitting about from idea to idea without processing it in our hearts or deducing the logic of it. Thus, Scripture calls us to discipline our hearts (2 Tim. 1:7). One of the most dangerous practices that sought to infiltrate the early church and continues in the church today is a philosophy of Gnosticism, or secret wisdom. Today we simply call it blind faith. The main attraction for this idea is that of a wisdom that only reveals its content to those who practice certain methods or reach certain spiritual heights. This practice is seen in the enthralling sensation of

---

[6] J. Gresham Machen, *What is Faith?* (Grand Rapids, MI: Eerdmans, 1965), 48.

worship music, babbling prayers, and Eastern meditation that has entered the evangelical church. But Hodge again helps, "Faith is not blind, irrational conviction. In order to believe, we must know what we believe, and the grounds on which our faith rests."[7] Let's be clear: the emotions we experience during our favorite worship song are not evidence of our faith, nor are they a means to save or justify us or anyone we know before God. As one pastor spoke to a congregation dealing with similar problems, "This is not the way you learned Christ" (Eph. 4:20). Our hearts have never taught us anything but deceit; we seek the heart of Christ who makes our hearts beat anew. Remember, faith comes by hearing the Word of God. We receive the content, fix our hearts upon it, and so exercise the received gift of saving faith.

Faith isn't leaping, it is learning ("By knowledge shall the chambers be filled with all precious and pleasant riches," Prov. 24:4). If we cannot discern what we believe, then we are passively stepping away from Scripture and how the Holy Spirit enlightens and strengthens those whom he regenerates. Truth isn't blind; God sanctifies us with knowable Truth (John 17:17), and by his working in us we synthesize affectionate knowledge of doctrine into obedience. Sanctification is the fancy word for growing and increasing in faith. Faith is indeed rational, logical, and yet mystical in its union. A single and continuous holy mysticism has happened in the sense that our humanly fallible eyes have become divinely infallible in how we receive the gospel.

---

[7] Hodge, *Systematic Theology*, 3:83.

How do we receive faith?

Illuminated by the Spirit

We are born again by the Spirit; through new eyes we seek after the propositions of Scripture and thereby mature in the gift of faith. Then what happens? Implanting of faith is nothing like secret wisdom. It is far more confounding, miraculous than what humans could contrive. The God of all creation gives self-revelation, gifting to our conscience an "absolutely reliable knowledge," while providing the source by which we are able to systematize and comprehend this revealing, accommodated for his creatures: the Bible.[8] A person goes from being initially dead to Scripture, but then is suddenly enlivened and passionate about its sacredness: only the intimate love of God can cause that change. The truths of the gospel are "peculiar, divine, supernatural." Therefore, to receive these truths which are necessary for salvation, God requires us and graciously gifts us "a peculiar, divine, supernatural habit, by which our minds may be enabled to receive."[9] We receive illumination in the gift of saving faith.

The best place to think about illumination is 1 Corinthians 2:3-15. This passage explains spiritual knowledge as a perpetual gifting based on the intimacy of being in union with Christ. Odd teachings and practices (Freemasonry, New Ageism, numerology, astrology, etc.) are attractive because they give a sense of importance, tantalize, and even seem like they have opened us to some new dimension. But they're really deluded

---

[8] Louis Berkhof, "Introductory Volume to Systematic Theology," in *Systematic Theology* (Carlisle, PA: Banner of Truth, 2021), 65. Berkhof explains that God gives his people *ectypal* knowledge. This is a helpful designation because we cannot know everything of God (the *archetypal* knowledge of himself which is impossible for the creature), but we do understand what he has chosen and given to us. We are capable, by grace, to learn and grow in the ectypal knowledge accommodated for us.

[9] John Owen, *An Exposition of the Epistle to the Hebrews*, vol. 4, *The Works of John Owen*, ed. W.H. Gould (1855; repr., Carlisle, PA: Banner of Truth, 1991), 247.

lies that purport God's chosen means is not enough, that God is holding out, that God's means is insufficient for the likes of us, as if God is trying but just can't get to those he loves. Scripture rightly divided teaches the mystery is revealed finally in the gospel (Rom. 16:25-27), not in secrecy or conjuring of saints. Scripture is the means of both receiving and maturing in faith. We need not seek after other human means but prioritize our primary means: the means of grace God has ordained for our receiving, increasing, and sharing the faith. We are illuminated *by* the Word and *for* the Word.

The gift of repentance
Because of our deadness in sin, our new heart has a lot of work to do in purging all the sinful desires and inclinations. We are born again, but we will continue to struggle and make progress in our holiness. So what do we do with all this growing faith in the propositions of Scripture? We put them to work to rid ourselves of attitudes and actions that are displeasing to our Lord! Regeneration is the syringe, faith is the vaccine, and repentance is the side effect.

We aren't called to punish ourselves; we were punished completely in the cross of Jesus Christ. Repentance is characterized as the "turning away" of a sinner from evil deeds unto good works. Thomas Brooks once said that repentance is a greater work in the Christian than never sinning at all. He remarks, "Repentance is the vomit of the soul,"[10] and scriptural propositions are our necessary ipecac—the at-times nausea-inducing medicine. By immersing ourselves in the Word of God, we are made to expel those parts and habits displeasing to God.

---

[10] Thomas Brooks, *Precious Remedies against Satan's Devices*, ed. Christopher Ellis Osterbrock (Peterborough, ON: H&E Publishing, 2020), 59.

If, in your heart, you feel conviction for patterns, habits, and past sins that you recognize as displeasing to God, drop what you're doing right then and pray to be purged of those things immediately (Prov. 16:6). Only when Christ is revealed to us can the corruption of sin be exposed and our intellect be changed.[11] Saving faith is the cause whose effect is repentance unto a life of sanctification—holy living. You will never desire to do good apart from the goodness of Christ's Spirit within you and your mind's proximity to the instruction of God's will.

The *Westminster Larger Catechism* shows the relationship of the Spirit and the Word in repentance. When we encounter Scripture, the Spirit will cause in us a desire to either blossom with obedience, prune with repentance, or more likely a mixture of both. Repentance is a grace, or fruit, that comes with the enlivening work of regeneration. "Saving repentance" is a result of being "made aware by the Holy Spirit of the many evils of [the believers'] sin."[12] Based on this awareness, repentance brings us before the throne of grace for pardon, perseverance, and replenishing power to do work for God.

Repentance is often seen as synonymous with saving faith; it is, after all, the most obvious fruit of faith and the first true exhibition of regeneration. These composite pieces are necessary for the whole to be real and true. No matter how lacking our education, saving faith is *saving* based on the propositions the Spirit inclines us to cling to for repentance. Our knowledge

---

[11] Thomas Joseph White, *The Incarnate Lord: A Thomistic Study in Christology* (Washington, D.C.: The Catholic University of America Press, 2017), 18. White writes, "only Christ can fully reveal to the human person what he or she is, or what he or she is made for ... the revelation of Christ must serve to correct multiple errors of the human intellect, both practical and speculative, that tend to corrupt fallen human thinking regarding what it means to be human."

[12] *WLC*, 76.

becomes affection, and godly affection produces repentance. Our conscience is conformed and forever changed by the gift of saving faith. Examine your inclinations now: is there repentance and affection pulsing in your heart?

Conclusion
We obtain the gift of faith by believing that the Holy Spirit has applied the promises of Jesus Christ found in Scripture, to us. You don't decide; if you could you never would. It's not the persuasion of a crafty salesman, not the tears you wept, not the altar call, not the amount of your belief or exertion, not the eloquence of your prayer, not the decision of your parent or priest, not even the nostalgia of some powerful event in your life; no, the reason you believe in the saving work of Christ and desire to live for him as Lord and Savior is because God chose to make the Holy Spirit dwell in you and seal you for his glory. That is a gift worth remembering! You'll always know the Giver because he himself is the gift. The infallible gift of faith is given to fallible people like us to infallibly seal us for his future glory. Knowing how this gift is received will dictate how it is assured, grown, and given to others. As we contemplate how we have received such a gift, our hearts inevitably will be stirred to ask: How can I *know* that I have received this gift? How can I be *sure* of my union with Christ?

How do we receive faith?

Examining our affections:

1. What does Paul's transformation look like in Acts 9:1-19? How did he receive salvation? Is this conversion unique to the Christian experience?
2. Summarize the term regeneration. What makes this word so important in talking about saving faith? Why is this word important when Christians explain faith alone and *not* works?
3. What is repentance? Why would God choose to intertwine faith and repentance? Explain how the process of repentance leads to joy.
4. Why ought Christians argue for Augustine's position, "Faith is gifted unasked for?" Why might some Bible reader's argue against it? What is a Scripture reference for the gifting of faith *and* what might be a reference used for the notion of faith as an accepting of Jesus into one's heart?
5. Why is the concept of "secret knowledge" antithetical to the church and dangerous to the gathering of Christians? How do we address the concern that gifting faith sounds a lot like "secret knowledge"?
6. How might you describe the importance of "propositions" to someone who does not hold to *saving* faith?

3
Can we be assured of our faith?

God's grip is more secure than a child's car seat. Last year, my wife was driving our small SUV by herself in the rain when a compact car ran straight into the back of her. Though everyone was fine, this collision necessitated replacing two very expensive car seats. Insurance covered it, but I remember my consternation looking at those car seats and the simple paint scuff on the bumper. How could a little collision like that ruin the warranty of these steel-frame harnesses? Then, I remember contemplating how more exponentially preposterous it is that the grip of the Savior's hand could ever be broken by a feeble man like me. If the omnipotent Son of God has his hand upon those the Father has chosen (John 10:26–30), how do we live in his grasp? That's our discussion in this chapter: how am I to live out the trust and assurance of saving faith?

Dependence on the object of faith
Saving faith is perplexing because of its connection with assurance. Someone may argue of a distinction between faith and the fulfillment of God's preservation. However, if God gives faith by indwelling us with his own co-eternal Spirit, then he does not take it away. This has serious ramifications in the Christian life. If faith is dependent on me, it can falter and is necessarily grounded on how I feel at any given moment; or is contingent on whether I have asked forgiveness for my most recent behaviors and idolatrous affections. But, Christian, there is no need of warranty for those sitting with Christ, purchased in his omnipotent blood. The deposit of faith is either timeless and

perfected in Christ, or it is bound by our time and as faulty as our holiness. Our faith is based on the object; we remember nothing of ourselves deserved his gracious deposit, but everything about the deposit points toward its future collection. He who promised is faithful (Heb. 10:23). The promise goes out to whoever the Father calls (John 6:37), and those he calls will be drawn perfectly and completely to Jesus Christ. Not a single person who has received his deposited promise will refuse him or be refused by him because he who is sovereign over salvation will lose none of those whom he has died for. They shall all be raised to see fully the gracious King Jesus in his glory and theirs (John 6:39–40, 44).

Assurance is based on the object of faith not on the recipient. John Colquhoun writes, "The object of the assurance of faith is Christ revealed and offered in the Word; the object of assurance of sense is Christ formed and perceived in the heart. The former is the root, and the latter is the fruit. The one is the cause, the other the effect."[1] Don't trust any sensation of assurance, trust the one who assures and let the senses remain tacitly human but trained toward holiness. Because the object is faithful, we trust that we are faithfully held by him, not of our own power or sensations. As Hodge puts it, "We believe on the authority of God, not because we see, know, or feel a thing to be true."[2]

Here is something difficult to discuss, but vitally important to our topic. If our assurance is based upon God's promises and abilities to hold poor sinners, to purify us and bring us into his home, then to doubt our assurance is to doubt him. Denying

---

[1] John Colquhoun, *A View of Saving Faith from the Sacred Records*, ed. Don Kistler (Orlando, FL: Northampton, 2008), 187.
[2] Charles Hodge, *Systematic Theology*, vol. 3 (Peabody, MA: Hendrickson, 2016), 61.

our assurance in faith is to doubt not only what God has promised, but to doubt the very concept and purpose of Christ's salvation. Now there is also a distinction to be made regarding false assurance, but we'll discuss that a bit more in the following chapter. We must hold to a biblical assurance that what Christ says is precisely what he does; otherwise he would be a liar.

God's faithfulness
Oddly enough, both the Hebrew and Greek terms used of our faith and faithfulness are used of God's faithfulness as well. What does it mean for our assurance that God is faithful? The opposite of faith for us is unbelief, for without believing we cannot enter the heavenly rest of Christ Jesus (Heb. 3:19). The opposite of a faithful God is one in whom we can place no trust, where there is marked failure and inability. Thus, we hold that God is sovereign in all he wills and fulfills. Deuteronomy 7:9 teaches that God is "the faithful God." Psalm 26:3 uses the same word, but it is translated as "true," and Psalm 33:4 shows "His work is done in faithfulness" or "His work is done in truth" (NKJV). The term is used to note confirmation, support, trust, and reliability. The faith we receive as a gracious gift for our regeneration is not possessed by us, but always indicative of a work produced by God. When we are born again, we are born into his truthfulness, confirmation, reliability, surety, stability, continuity of his character—unchangingness, immutability (Num. 23:19; Isa. 25:1). Jesus, who saves us, is marked in 1 Corinthians 1:9 as the fulness, or fulfillment of our faith—through him we see fulfillment of what was promised

and the substance of all the Old Testament claims.[3]

Faithfulness, as we've described, is related to diligence in what ought to be believed. What is to be believed of God remains steadfast and true. For us, faithfulness is a perpetual desire to know the truth of the doctrines and propositions of our object of faith—to see biblical propositions as the only salve for sufferings, the only fruit for feasting, and the only seeds for sowing. Faithful Christians aren't hanging on the wing of the plane; they are harnessed to the truth that withstands turbulence. We do not have crises of faith, but providential experiences for self-examination, to bring us back to our object of faith. Though you will despair, doubt, challenge, and at times grow cold in your obedience, if you are sealed in Christ, he will hold you fast. If you're *not* in Christ, be concerned for your faith. If you *are* in Christ, be concerned for your faithfulness, but motivated by his.

Obedience or application or experience

When I use the term *experience* regarding faith, what picture comes to your mind? For most Christians we have an expectation that is wildly divergent from the biblical picture of faithfulness. When I think of Christian experience, my own inclinations lead me to think of beatific visions, the dead raised *literally*, and those ecstatic emotions I so rarely sense in myself. What if we're categorically getting our experience of faithfulness wrong? We're not called to blindly love Jesus as much as we can, we're called to be absorbed in the truths he has shared with us and love him because of what we can know of him. Because saving faith is affectionate knowledge of scriptural

---

[3] This is the same language used for "trustworthy" in 1 Corinthians 7:25 and "He who calls you is faithful," in 1 Thessalonians 5:24.

truths, obedience in spiritual growth is best wrought in applying God's truths to our daily lives. Obedience, as an evidence of faith, is pictured biblically as faithfulness. The argument for a clear doctrine of saving faith is an argument that experience isn't determined by human sensations but is the holistic obedience of applying God's word. Therefore, the experience, whether positive or negative, sheer bliss or anxious trial, is a challenge for our growth in application of God's word—in efforts toward obedience in faith. Though Satan could very easily use a flat tire on some rainy evening as a trial to make me curse and make everyone around me miserable, so in obedience the same trial can be turned to an experience of union with my Savior as I restrain my emotions by applying God's Word in obedience.

Obedience is an active experience of spirituality. Learning to apply God's truth is an active experience of the Spirit working through our faith. We experience the faith-increasing, faith-maturing, faith-saturating doctrines and revelation of God; we do so through spiritual disciplines and discipleship within the local church. This is true faithfulness. The love of God is directly connected to our walking in obedience, to abiding in the study of Christian doctrines (2 John 1:6, 9). We are called to grow in the word and in its application, not blindly in our zeal or in some passive emotional experience—such things only pull us farther away from the object of our faith. We could never be sure of your salvation, or even attempt assurance if we are basing faith upon our own subjective grounds. Assurance is as solid and unchanging as Scripture.

Christ the shepherd leads and nourishes his flock in the green pastures of Scripture no matter the sunshine, rain, or dark of this world. And by their abiding in this ever-present feast, the shepherd assures his flock of his presence with them here and hereafter. May we, his flock, use whatever means afforded us to increase our faith in his abiding presence by doing that which takes his word, impresses it to us, and affects our hearts.

Nostalgic deception

Nostalgic deception, in my observation, is the demise of many well-intentioned evangelistic efforts in the evangelical church, as illustrated in the ministry of Charles Finney (1792–1875). Finneyism, or American revivalism, is a philosophy of winning responses. Here we are distinguishing true revival initiated by the Holy Spirit, invigorating those churches who had grown complacent or stagnant, with what can be called humanly manufactured revivalism. Finney was so good at getting his hearers fired up and fostering an atmosphere of fervor that he put together a manual for these "new measures" of evangelism. This manual explained how to conduct revival services to manipulate people into having emotional episodes, calling on them to raise their hands or answer an altar call (an invention of Finney's), and then proving his own success by counting all the souls. Many a preacher, even ignorant to the origins, has followed what are called "new measures" and found they had the right personality, right songs, or right method to get people to respond to an experience and even get them to give lots of money to the facilitators of that experience.[4]

---

[4] Iain H. Murray, *Revival & Revivalism: The Making and Marring of American Evangelicalism 1750-1858* (Carlisle, PA: Banner of Truth, 1994), 261. The greatest book on understanding the difference between a biblical revival versus revivalism, and the best answer as to why evangelicalism has lately left so many once churched people now wandering outside the church.

Can we be assured?

    The greatest challenge, and an entirely avoidable one, is the false sense of security provided for those who have an emotional response and then assume they are saved. This is a cheap grace offered by false doctrine, holding that the object of faith is an ethereal, subjective psychological effect. This is a human product, a concert mentality—that a person has seen or witnessed something at a point in time and can look back on it fondly as if memory is salvific. If it was how someone came to think themselves saved, then why wouldn't it be the best option for everyone else? But it is a deception; it is repeatable by many other religions. These "new measures" offer no growth in biblical doctrine. Herein we observe the language of "acceptance" demonstrates the subjective nature of our faith, whereas the far more biblical language of assent shows the objective gifting of God's grace. When a person comes to faith on the rocky path, or the shallow soil, or growing amongst the thorns and thistles how could they withstand the promised circumstances without the soil of healthy doctrine? When despair inevitably comes, they will quickly ask the important question, "was I ever saved at all?" And, with shallow doctrine, they will run to whatever church looks attractive and feels comfortable and safe. Thus, the process has been repeated in American evangelicalism over the last fifty years. The foundation of such faith is not Jesus Christ but emotion, personality, the context and culture of time spent in the proverbial tent. Revivalism leaves people counted, but not saved.

    I've called it nostalgic deception because, even if the false faith has failed, we long for what we thought about it at the time. We want to deceive ourselves, that what we liked best at that moment was worthwhile and truly saving. We think we must have messed it up, yet we believe in ourselves enough to think we still know best. In my limited experience, people want a subjective experience to be their anchor of hope. In our earthly world that is what makes sense. We want to look to a point on a map of our personal story; we say this is where and when it happened, and we seek to recreate this context as a means for spiritual growth. But that is not the case. Salvation is not a point on the map, but a union with the Christ who saves regardless of any place you are on your map. Experience is secondary to growth, and growth happens by application, and application happens when we obey doctrine no matter the context.

Obedience as experience (again)

Saving faith is not connected to context or experience, but to Jesus Christ. Whether the pastor evidences moral failure, the song gets old, the church can rid itself of gossip, or we personally stumble in our progress, yet Jesus Christ is the same yesterday, today, and forever—he is the substance of our faith. Our faith is given to us no matter the stuff attached to it in the moment. But we must remind ourselves, the evidence of our faith is in how we handle the circumstances we come into, whether they are positive or negative. Our obedience doesn't give us certainty, but our certainty in Christ motivates our obedience. John MacArthur once quipped, "I don't look for a past event to make my salvation real to me. I look at the present pattern of my life."[5] If I am assured of salvation, then I will necessarily live in a way to experience my faith. If we want stability in our faith, it must not be dependent on ourselves, but entirely on Christ, the object of our faith. Stability comes through

---

[5] John MacArthur, *Saved Without a Doubt: Being Sure of Your Salvation*, 2nd ed. (Colorado Springs, CO: Victor, 2006), 118.

application. Let us not be deceived by such failing nostalgia, but instead depend upon the never-failing God who has been and will continue to be sovereign over every circumstance and experience.

The infallible faith of God
Without coming right out and saying a saved person is permanently saved, let's look at it a different way. Instead of at the human side, perhaps we ought to be gazing at what God has revealed. If Christ assures our faith, we are infallibly assured.[6] Question eighty of the *Westminster Larger Catechism* reads,

> Such as truly believe in Christ, and endeavour to walk in all good conscience before him, may, without extraordinary revelation, by faith grounded upon the truth of God's promises, and by the Spirit enabling them to discern in themselves those graces to which the promises of life are made be infallibly assured.

Though we may wait a long time to obtain a real sense of our assurance, or experience incredible weakness and "manifold distempers, sins, temptations, and desertions," yet we "are never left without such a presence and support of the Spirit of God as keeps [us] from sinking into utter despair."[7] Once again, we remember that our experience of assurance is fallible, but God's faithfulness in preserving those in whom his Spirit rests is eternally trustworthy. Our sensations are human, but his saving is divine.

---

[6] "The Larger Catechism," in *The Westminster Confession* (Carlisle, PA: Banner of Truth, 2018), 244.
[7] *WCF*, 245. This is part of the response to question #81.

There is no faith gland in our bodies producing affection for Jesus Christ. Even in biblical language, the production and perpetual conviction associated with faith are direct results of God's gracious deposit. To translate it in a way that might be a bit more memorable: "Lord, I faith; help my inabilities in faithing." And again, "Lord, increase our faith" (Mark 9:24; Luke 17:5). I like the way one commentator on Herman Bavinck put it, "Certainty flows from faith spontaneously," that is, we place our faith in the certainty of who God is and not according to the humanness involved, but independent of the human — just as logically as saving grace is independent of the human.[8] Don't go looking *for* an experience, start looking *at* the means for experience, therein lies assurance. True saving faith is a golden path to look backwards with genuine joy, not nostalgic deception. Jesus will surprise us by his intimacy with us even in the mundanity of life.

Growing in assurance

Our assurance is based on the object of our faith not on our fallible degree to which we *feel* assured. Our degree of assurance is directly connected to our assent to and affections for who Jesus Christ is.[9] Therefore, we must hasten to grow in doctrinal, theological knowledge![10] Our affections are raised as we raise our mind to scriptural truth. If we want to know our position before the throne of God, to be confident and bold (Heb. 4:16), then we're to grow in the doctrines of Jesus Christ, the truths enlivened in us by the word and work of the Spirit. We are to

---

[8] Henk van den Belt, "Herman Bavinck's Lectures on the Certainty of Faith (1891)," in *Bavinck Review* 8 (2017): 49.
[9] Colquhoun, *A View of Saving Faith*, 194-196.
[10] Colquhoun, *A View of Saving Faith*, 196.

have a compulsion to grow in faithfulness and not be stagnant in our experience of God's grace.

Conclusion

Those in Christ will exhibit a compulsion, a propensity, an affection, not only to grow in knowledge but in affection lived out through obedience that points heavenward. Our assurance is grown as we grow in learning the truths of God's Word. Gordon Clark explains that we do not have a minimum because we do not have a maximum number of faith-invigorating propositions—that's the beauty of an infallible, inestimable object of faith.[11] Our assurance will continue to be bolstered throughout the Christian life, acknowledging within ourselves that we are always in want, yet Christ will unfathomably supply and sustain our need of intimacy with him. Our faith has no warranty; the Lord's grip is secure forever.

---

[11] Gordon H. Clark, *Faith and Saving Faith*, 2nd ed. (Jefferson, MD: Trinity Foundation, 1990), 109.

Examining our affections:

1. Describe how obedience, faith, and assurance relate as an equation for our spiritual life?
2. How would you explain God's faithfulness to a non-believer? How would you explain the connection between application, obedience, and experience? How might understanding experience as a fruit of application/obedience help us prevent dangerous ideas?
3. Have you clung to an experience as your moment of faith? Explain how this could derail spiritual growth.
4. What is nostalgic deception? How does such an idea infect the church? Have you observed any kinds of "experience-based" traditions in your church life that may be categorized as nostalgic deception? How so? What is a solution, or alternative, to strengthen or graciously correct your local church against this mindset?
5. How does infallible assurance strengthen your faith journey and motivate obedience? What are you currently doing to grow in your assurance?
6. Why do we so often look to benefits, rather than God? How might this negatively affect our assurance and/or personal spiritual growth?

4
How do we defend against false faith?

The brilliant composer Robert Schumann wrote, in a letter to Johann Hummel, "I can play every concerto at sight, but, fundamentally speaking, must begin with the C major scale."[1] Taking our queue from Schumann, where do we begin in our spiritual life? No matter if we can play theology, spirituality, or doctrine "at sight," all our best efforts ought to start by first going back to the scale of the Bible and hearing from those three magnificent guides: book, chapter, verse. Fundamentally speaking, when it comes to our faith, we must always be tracing our actions and motivations back to the object of our faith. We are to make sure and evident the source and object of our faith. Remember what 1 Corinthians 4:6 cautions us, dear Christian, "that [we] may learn ... not to go beyond what is written." Even when it comes to what we think we know about God, we must be a people who meditate on doctrines, revealing to ourselves whether they are logical and discernable in the scriptural account of God, for the purpose of growing our affections in Jesus Christ. After all, our faith is not ethereal; it has a substance (Heb. 12:2).

Our task now is to be able to defend ourselves and others against false faiths—those beliefs or influences that pull us from sound doctrine. The means of defense begins with our own self-examination regarding false faith influences. Only after we have exposed what may be questionable within ourselves

---

[1] Robert Schumann, *Schumann on Music: A Selection from the Writings*, ed. Henry Pleasants (New York: Dover, 1988), 26n1. This is in a letter dated August 31, 1831.

can we come along to help others defend against those things as well. Our goal in defending against false faith is not to destroy other people, but to maintain our evangelistic perspective against vice, to save those lost under Satan's sway. So how do we begin with our own self-examination?

Preparing for examination
Because faith is not blind—we have a substantive object of faith—we cannot be satisfied in our spiritual health unless it will stand the scrutiny of self-examination. Those growing in faith will be a people who can examine and find that they are rooted in the doctrines delivered down from the saints. We are called to test, not only the spirits, but the doctrines we encounter and, just as much, the affections that stir within us.

I love Sherlock Holmes stories; part of the reason is his cold, articulate, and often maddeningly simple procedure of deduction. Like Schumann, he traces the action back to the source. He doesn't get carried away by the irrational elements, or personal impulses, because he never lets them confuse the facts that lead to his solution (you might say, salvation). The Bible calls us to be Holmesian deducers of saving faith: "Examine yourselves, to see whether you are in the faith. Test yourselves. Or do you not realize this about yourselves, that Jesus Christ is in you?—unless indeed you fail to meet the test!" (2 Cor. 13:5). By testing, not only ourselves, but others, we will grow in knowledge and the spiritual gift of discernment.

Not everything spiritual is from God, not every inclination we might receive. Surely, we remember that our own hearts are deceitful (Jer. 17:9), that's why we seek after Christ within us (2 Cor. 3:15). We are called to "test the spirits," that which is around us urging us one way or another, for by testing against

How do we defend against false faith?

Scripture we will grow in the Spirit of truth and destroy the spirit of error (1 John 4:1, 6). We ought not allow for our spiritual health to be decentralized, but "in all our ways acknowledge him" (Prov. 3:6). Following our continuous examination, we can collect those unsound parts of us, purge them, and be ready to come against them in future experiences.

Beware of impulses and impressions
At times I have opened my Bible and attempted to insert my own idea into a verse. There's even been times where I've wanted God to speak to me, or I've fervently prayed to see glorious sights. I've picked up the Bible and opened randomly to receive special "text messages" from Jesus. These emotional exertions are quite easy habits for us to fall into. But none of these exercises are prescribed to us. Sometimes we go to these exercises because we've become intimidated with the big words of religion, but most of the time it's because we don't want to ruin the version we've embraced—we've taken our personal experiences as the concrete foundation of our belief system even though we know that we're in a very dangerous place. A person doesn't have to submit to the authority of Scripture if they've fabricated their own personal journey as the ultimate dogma for their life. If that's the case, then they don't even need to read Scripture or endure a Sunday service, because, however erringly illogical, that's not where they learned their version of Jesus (Eph. 4:20).

Andrew Fuller wrote that "we must not deal in curious speculations, which have no foundation in the Scriptures. Some have turned aside by such an indulgence to false hypotheses and made a shipwreck of faith and a good conscience."[2] There is a kind of speculation that is always grievous; it cannot help but be so. This is the speculation regarding how God reveals himself. Children will inevitably ask, "Who made God?" and this is healthy; it is the beginning of abstract thought, and a pleasant discussion will likely follow. But when we start speculating about our own ideas or things we have heard, we conflate folklore with propositions of Christ and sound doctrine (2 Tim. 4:3). We do not rest our faith on speculation. All spiritual knowledge ought to point us to the greater glory of God. Fuller shares again, "We must not deal in private impulses or impressions, which have no foundation in the Scriptures. One founds a doctrine on his own experience; but experience ought to be judged by the Bible, not the Bible by experience." The keywords here are impulses and impressions, but notice he does not include the category *interpretation*. We are called to grow in a diligent, studious theological interpretation of certain texts. In his sovereign knowledge of us, the Lord even wills us to take an impulse or personal impression about a theological idea and make it obedient to Christ through our examination of Scripture (2 Cor. 10:5). But to seek after strange ideas, to desire to fashion our own impulses as authoritative, to manipulate Scripture, or even disregard Scripture is to indeed shipwreck faith. In these instances, we are actively forming another religion, not clinging to a systematic understanding of Jesus Christ.

There are plenty of safeguards for our impulses found within our creeds and confessions. These helpful fences, aligned according to Scripture, protect us and help us test our

---

[2] David E. Prince, *Preaching the Truth as It Is in Jesus: A Reader on Andrew Fuller* (Peterborough, ON: H&E Publishing, 2022), 44.

own thoughts against an organized scope of the Holy Bible. My ministry has taught me that many well-meaning individuals may be completely unaware of the church history packed into those ancient creeds and defining confessions. Phrases like "I think" followed by ideas and speculations show a hungry person seeking to digest Scripture rightly. Others may claim "no creed, but Christ!" But when asked further concerning views on baptism or eldership and we could unpack a healthy document's worth of confessions concerning how to interpret Scripture. Church history offers the wisdom of others who have been tempted in similar ways. We would be wise to learn and remember this is history is our own.

One instance that continues to trouble the church regarding impulses has to do with spiritism (involving angels, visions, and ghosts). Even many who have been lifelong church members desire to be entertained with ideas and hopes of encountering these strange manifestations. These elements are no different than the Gnosticism pervasive during the first century, which was taught against in many of the New Testament epistles (as we noted in the previous chapter).[3] Belief in ghosts (spiritualism or necromancy), mysterious or secret wisdom, and visions of saints or guardians is contrary to an understanding of salvation in Jesus Christ and serves to corrupt the orthodox doctrines of heaven, hell, and the role of Christ in judgment. Those who do so are at the very least seeking to obtain special wisdom or entertainment from the realm of God, yet apart from him.

---

[3] My short answer when prodded on the subject: you have no ghost or apparition, but a demonic presence seeking to confuse and distract you from union with Jesus Christ. The only ghost in Scripture, the witch of Endor (1 Samuel 28), was certainly not a prescriptive account, nor was it indicative of a systematic understanding of the topic. John Gill has rightly understood the representation of Samuel in this passage as merely a deception from Satan, as we know full well the goodness of God had left Saul and Samuel was in the paradise that is with Christ.

This points to a few deeper issues: a motivation to go beyond Christ's will, and an affection separate from his glory. Our examination, our willingness and humility to test our impulses and inclinations, will reveal whether we are following spiritualism or biblical spirituality.

Spiritualism or biblical spirituality
Adding humanly fashioned spirituality to what God has ordained can be traced back at least as far as Leviticus 10:1–2. Nadab and Abihu, two sons of Aaron, observed the practices of the priests and heard the particulars concerning worship in the tabernacle. In their zeal to worship, when and how they thought would be best, they brought a sacrifice when God had not spoken. They brought "strange fire" before the Lord, and he consumed them entirely. Their presumption points to a lack of affections for who Jesus is as he revealed himself. It is as if we are saying, "I don't want what God reveals. I want something special to me, that empowers my own experiences."

Our zeal to be spiritual, to grow in religion as we think best, is a problem if not directed according to Scripture. There is a big difference between the use of the term *spiritual* in the Bible and the way it is used by the world. If *spiritual* concerns the Holy Spirit, our union with Christ, and the things of God, then I am not the one in charge of what is spiritual. I am not capable of manipulating spiritual things, but submissive and resigned to how the Spirit orders spiritual matters to be understood—he is, after all, the same triune God. When we focus our zeal, even if contrary to our inclinations, we are headed toward pleasing and glorifying God—deferring to the Spirit's chosen means of obtaining intimacy with our Savior.

How do we defend against false faith?

As we examine our faith, we ask the question, how do I defend against bringing strange fire before the Lord, worshipping him in a way he never asked or desired? Jonathan Edwards (1703-1758) wrote on this subject voraciously,

> When persons' affections are founded on imaginations, which is often the case, those affections are merely natural and common, because they are built on a foundation that is not spiritual, and so are entirely different from gracious affections, which, as has been proved, do evermore arise from those operations that are spiritual and divine.[4]

Notice Edwards speaks of the term *spiritual* in the biblical manner. Our defense of faith is tested by our affections for that which the Spirit teaches us in the Word. In the following two sections we will examine our affections—testing our likeness to Nadab and Abihu. But we will do so understanding that there are two sides to this spiritual battle, to lean into ecstatic, personal passions or to lean into cold, stoic intellectualism.

Against strange fire: emotionalism

I once had a church member who suffered a stroke and was not doing well at all. I happened to be in the hospital, praying with the family. It was not my best prayer, by a long shot. But during that time, she happened to flatline, we continued praying and she was healed. A month later she and her family were back in our Sunday services. Not long after, a couple with close ties to the family, but from a charismatic church, came to visit our building. One said to me, as compliment, "you must have immense faith to be able to bring her back. Thank God you were

---

[4] Jonathan Edwards, *The Religious Affections* (Carlisle, PA: Banner of Truth, 2007), 145.

there to pray." This took me by surprise for several reasons that speak to the issue of faith: first, were the prayers of the family not good enough for God? Second, was God dependent on my amount of faith to work such miracles? Third, would I have been at fault had I not prayed for her? Fourth, would God have been wrong, according to the praise I received, to pass that woman through death? Fifth, what will be said when my prayers *aren't* answered the way I desire? We'll get to some of these issues in the following chapter.

The kind of faith represented in this idea of answered prayer shows a lot of similarities with Nadab and Abihu, as well as the prophets of Baal who raved and screamed to conjure or manipulate a blessing from their deity (1 Kngs 18:20–40). Heightened emotionalism gives the elusive promise that God is either dependent on how *hard* we believe or requires a particular offering before he will act. This mentality suggests our fervency will win reward; the Spirit is perpetually assessing our fervor or sensations as though they were in proportion to a blessing or breakthrough. Therefore, the veracity of our faith is contingent on how well we are sensing God and conjuring his favor. Are the affections of the object of faith present in this kind of prayer? Can sound doctrine be extracted from the phrase, "you must have immense faith in order to make them come back to life"? We can boil down this kind of faith into a single word: sensationalism.

A faith rooted in our own sensations will always be lacking, unstable, given to waxing and waning, and never satisfying. But a saving faith will provide a foundation whichis incomprehensible to the sensationalism the world seeks. The Baptist theologian Anne Dutton (1692–1765) speaks of her conversion as being accompanied by the struggles of sensationalism:

How do we defend against false faith?

I too much lived upon enjoyments, I delighted to have my interest in Christ tried, by all the marks and signs of a believer, which were continually laid down in the ministry. When I could find them, my heart was filled with joy; but, if there were any I did not clearly discern, I sunk down in sorrow. So foolish was I, that I looked for the effects of faith, when faith was not in exercise. ... No! the soul that enters into rest by faith, must have somewhat more firm and stable, than fleeting frames to lean upon. I began to rejoice in my dear Lord Jesus as always the same, even when my frames were altered. Thus the Lord began to establish me, and settle my faith upon its proper basis: [the person Jesus Christ].[5]

She gets to the heart of our dilemma perfectly. Sensation would always fail her in the reality of the Christian experience. Dutton is speaking of a saving faith—and evidencing her journey toward this doctrine as she examines herself. Saving faith accounts for struggle because the seat of affections isn't based in us, but in the object of our faith: Jesus Christ. He is leading us away from trusting our sensations or feeble faith, that we may trust in him and his eternity instead.

We are tried by truth and tempered in grace. That is how we discern if our ideas or impressions go against what the Lord has revealed. We should test every idea, whether we're so confident we can "play it at sight"; we are to be sure we aren't going "against the knowledge of God" (2 Cor. 10:15). We are called to the defense of the gospel (Phil. 1:16) and to take no part, but expose whatever is not regulative, contingent, and

---

[5] Anne Dutton, "A Narration of the Wonders of Grace," in *Selected Spiritual Writings of Anne Dutton: Eighteenth Century, British-Baptist, Woman Theologian*, ed. Joann Ford Watson (Macon, GA: Mercer, 2004), 2:84–86.

deduced according to the Word (Eph. 5:11). We are to be latched as bondservants to the revealed canon of Scripture.

Against strange ice: cerebralism
For, Particular Baptists like myself, our cerebralism is too often our crutch. Many who have been deemed cold or unemotional, stoic or cynical, are often seeking to preserve doctrine to the fault of forgetting about the wonder and majesty of experimental faith; we are to experiment the spiritual life according to sound doctrine.

Cerebralism is a term that means we give far too much emphasis on knowledge and too little on practice. But we know that "even the demons believe—and shudder" (Jas. 2:19), this is precisely why we refer to faith as an *affectionate* knowledge, something more than facts and memory. Affections drive us to live differently, to no longer be conformed to this world, to not only believe the things of God, but desirous about who God is and how he is redeeming us. Is he the subject and object of worship? False faith will show up most clearly in our worship, not by whether we're sincere, but whether we're biblical practitioners. Does cerebralism effect our grace in family worship, our intimacy and leadership or submission to our spouse, our evangelism, our singing or creative worship before the Father, our ability to move from intellect to application? All these circumstances are places to thrive in *affectionate* knowledge—to live in his saving faith. The key here: we're not merely pursuing knowledge, but grounded affections for our Savior and Lord.

Knowledge is not an excuse for laxity in practice or passion. As Thomas Manton notes concerning Cain, "the faith that had an influence upon his sacrifice was faith in the general rewards and compensations of religion."⁶ Obviously we would never count such a faith as saving. The object of Cain's faith was not Christ (or a prefigured understanding of God's redemption), but it was the prosperity he would have had if he lived a certain way. Either Cain's knowledge or his feelings, he believed, would generate some reward. Emotionalism receives the brunt of accusations concerning a reward mentality (health, wealth, prosperity), but there is just as much of a pride and reward issue in cerebralism. Knowledge without affection for Christ will never please the Father. All knowledge of who Jesus Christ is must compel us, if it is indeed a *saving* faith, toward a spiritual art of putting affection into practice. Of "working out salvation" by training our affections to move us to obedience, as Christ was obedient even to the point of crucifixion (Phil. 2:12-13).

Regulative not speculative

As I scroll social media, sometimes I'll see advertisements for the Red Bull Flugtag, an annual event in over 30 cities, where men and women build these strange contraptions they pretend have a chance at flight. It's obvious these crafts are only meant for a laugh as contestants ride their vessels across a plank into a lake. This event is a stark reminder that if folks really want to fly, they would use the regular means of flight, what gets a person to a destination safely. Does our practice of worship, and method for receiving and growing in faith, look like a craft meant to carry us to a safe destination before the presence of almighty God? Do we practice the regulative means that God has ordained for worship? Or does our profession and

---

⁶ Thomas Manton, *By Faith: Sermons on Hebrews 11* (Carlisle, PA: Banner of Truth, 2000), 144.

understanding of faith lived through us and our religious practices look more like the faith of a Red Bull contraption?

When Jonathan Edwards was watching his church exhibit strange new sensations and signs during the first Great Awakening he sought to analyze Scripture to point him to a reason for these psychological manifestations. The revival was wonderful—his and the surrounding churches saw vast numbers of converts—yet he wanted to interview and hear if true gospel-centered salvation was grasped in all the faculties of these souls. He wrote shortly after,

> a work is not to be judged of by any effects on the bodies of men; such as tears, tremblings, groans, loud outcries, agonies of body, or the failing of bodily strength. The influence persons are under is not to be judged of one way or other by such effects on the body; and the reason is because the Scripture nowhere gives us any such rule.[7]

The regular means for revival is simply the Holy Spirit choosing to invigorate men and women as they grow in his gift of faith, the faithful affection for him. Surely, we ought to be praying fervently for such revival.

We live by faith, not by sight. Yes, but though we do not see the object of our faith now, we have received the complete rule for our doctrines and practices. Even his Spirit has chosen to embolden us and test us according to the written Word. Speculation does not lead to affections for Christ to be glorified and loved by his church, not unless it is a mere tool submissive under Scripture. When we test ourselves according to the principles in Scripture that shepherd us to treat worship and personal

---

[7] Jonathan Edwards, *On Revival* (Carlisle, PA: Banner of Truth, 1995), 91.

How do we defend against false faith?

disciplines within certain guides, we may feel restricted and convicted, but this is for our good because it is for his glory—training our affections for him as he trains our impulses and impressions to submit to him as Lord.

Our best defense
We are called to defend against false faith by the Word dwelling in us richly, by knowing the object of faith according to a standard. Our best defense may indeed make us and others uncomfortable, but that is precisely what conviction does as it grows the body both in depth and in soul-winning. Our defense is offered not as our word—we're not the one making a person uncomfortable or agitated—but as God's revelation. He can defend himself through the Scripture, so let him. (After all, Scripture is his chosen means to bring his people to salvation, do we trust him enough to let him speak?) Our task is to make clear and precise the truth of God's revelation, especially if false impulses and impressions are coming against what is revealed. Are we prepared to destroy arguments and the lofty ideas that challenge the scriptural knowledge of the triune God (2 Cor. 10:5)? The means to increase our faith is the same means to purge us, and the church, of false faith. We must go back to examine if we truly believe in a *saving* faith, if our affections are stirred for the knowledge that comes by Scripture. The more we saturate ourselves in the Word of God, the deeper we will grow no matter our circumstances or context. Feelings are a far greater threat to our sanctification than suffering or discomfort ever could be. Suffering is not an indication of weak or feeble faith—just the opposite. Suffering is a means given for spiritual growth not just in pruning but in developing greater resolve and union with Christ.

Conclusion

Defending against false faith means setting aside our own inclinations and impulses. This isn't easy, but the blessings through the process will affect not only ourselves but our church and those around us. When Robert Schumann went back to that C Major scale he proved himself capable of doing far more than most pianists at the time. When our churches go back to God's Word, God himself will prove his Word within us. The more we invest in the truths as presented in Jesus Christ, the more comfort and shelter we can provide for those who have been led out into the heat and danger of the desert sun. The church is the deep pool, the oasis for strangers and pilgrims. We must be that tree planted by streams of living water[8] and those around us will sense their thirst and be drawn by the Shepherd's voice living in his church. We want to be grown in the right faith, but what does it mean to be grown? When our faith is increased,[9] is it by us or by the Lord? Let's dig into that question in the next chapter.

---

[8] Psalm 1:3.
[9] Luke 17:5.

How do we defend against false faith?

Examining our affections:

1. How would you categorize your inclinations when it comes to the issue of faith? Do you lean toward "strange fire" or "strange ice"? Explain.
2. What is meant when we use the word *regulative*? How might this word be used in formulating a view for church practice? What is the alternative practice? When is what is not *regulative* deemed an "acceptable" act of worship?
3. Have you ever experienced an argument concerning how Christians are to worship? What sort of practices do you find to be revealed in Scripture? How might we approach those who step outside our comfort zone with worship?
4. Why is examination such a vital part of Christian spiritual health? Describe how you might organize a time of examination or reflection.
5. In conversation about speculative things in Scripture, the ideas of ghosts, visions, impressions, or feelings about decisions, how might these things benefit or corrupt a biblical understanding of salvation, saving faith, or doctrines of heaven and hell?
6. Explain how growing in understanding and protecting a certain biblical view might help a person grow and lead others to greater spiritual vitality.

5
How can I practice my faith?

By a simple look to the ostrich, we understand that it isn't wings that make something soar, but when a bird *is* soaring, those wings are absolutely essential. Likewise, Christians aren't gifted faith by accident. Faith transforms those to whom it is gifted. Over the last two chapters we've observed the obedience that accompanies saving faith. How do we comprehend the incomprehensible God working in us and through us?

The antidote to depravity—our winglessness—is both justification *and* sanctification. God makes us saved *and* makes us capable of holiness. He doesn't just gift us wings, but he offers us the sky and the power to stay in it—to live for the new creation while yet in the present wilderness.

There's a particular Grateful Dead song that brings me to think of saving faith in this way. The *Attics of My Life* reads in part,

> I have spent my life
> seeking all that's still unsung
> Bent my ear to hear the tune
> and closed my eyes to see
> When there were no strings to play
> You played to me
>
> When I had no wings to fly
> You flew to me

Robert Hunter explains he was meditating on the concept of grace as he penned this poem.[1] He does give some hints at truth here at how grace *could* enter a dead sinner. However, these hints do not lead anyone to regeneration because Hunter was not a professing believer—he did not understand real transformative grace. I love this song, but it is marred by its incompleteness. There is within it an apathy for spiritual growth and discipline; there's no significant resolution. Someone who was depraved is suddenly "born again" into a new way of merely passive living. Though it's a pretty sentiment, from our theological perspective, it falls short. When we had no wings to fly, he flew to us. But Hunter, now we have wings! Now we call out, "Lord, teach us to fly in your power." And the Lord calls us to fly with him. If faith is a gift, then we are to experience real growth in it, real change from it, and real joy out of it. So how do we practice saving faith?

Born to grow
Andrew Fuller taught that faith is "an act of God of which the sinner is not immediately conscious."[2] But it doesn't end there; we're called to progressively grow in our conformity to Christ—the object of our faith and the basis for our joyful presence before God. Fuller continues, once saving faith is born and the regenerate sinner can know the fullness of God's will and desires, it is that faith that compels, that gives proclivity to cling more and more upon the truths of Scripture and so crawl

---

[1] Robert Hunter, "Attics of My Life," in *The Complete Annotated Grateful Dead Lyrics: The Collected Lyrics of Robert Hunter and John Barlow, Lyrics to All Original Songs, with Selected Traditional and Cover Songs*, ed. David Dodd and Alan Trist (New York, NY: Simon & Schuster, 2015), 116. In the spirit of full disclosure, I'm a deadhead (though without the mind-altering aspects of the culture).

[2] Robert W. Oliver, *History of the English Calvinistic Baptists, 1771-1892 from John Gill to C.H. Spurgeon* (Carlisle, PA: Banner of Truth, 2006), 154.

more and more toward perfect obedience (Rom. 16:25-27). Jesus said, "If anyone would come after me, let him deny himself and take up his cross daily and follow me. For whoever would save his life will lose it, but whoever loses his life for my sake will save it."³ Clearly the act of God gifts us more than mere wings, but the power of flight necessary to experience those wings.

My older daughters, three and six as of this writing, have a bin full of multi-colored blocks stored neatly in a shelf. Occasionally they will run over and pour all the blocks on the floor in their playroom; the older of the two will begin cautiously erecting a tower, ever mindful of her younger sister who is prone to knock over any nearby structure. The gift of faith is much like the gift of blocks. As a "good" father, those two girls are my own and I desire for them to experience the blocks I've provided, to enjoy and learn from their experiences. I especially intend for them to build blocks in my presence, even with me. Just as well, no matter what they seek to build, the first block of any structure is already laying there on the floor. Even if the storms of life—or a mischievous sibling—come to wreck the blocks of faith, there is an assured base upon which to rebuild. These girls are born to grow in my presence, to be mature, healthy, and joyfully obedient. The same is true of us as regenerated members in the body of Christ. The first step in practicing faith is to recognize our newness: the faith that has awakened us and draws us to substance in life is a compelling faith that moves us to be greater than we are.

---

³ Luke 9:23-24.

Compelled by affections

Herman Bavinck preached a sermon where he identified a few of the "glorious features of faith," from 1 John 5:4. He wrote,

> First, faith implants a new beginning of life within a person. In addition, John testifies that faith in Jesus as the Christ, is a mighty power for the love and obedience to God's commands. And the experience of this unbounded love compels him to love with all his soul and mind and strength the one who gave him birth.[4]

Unbounded love is the source for our ability to practice soaring in the skies of God. Practicing faith is never about my best life now; it is always about God's glory now and forevermore. All that we do is to be reckoned according to our affections in pleasing and living for Christ. What we do that does not correspond to affectionate knowledge of scriptural truths is regarded as sin, "for whatever does not proceed from faith is sin" (see Rom. 14:22-23). God gifts us to be the example of his glory on earth. He does this, not by results focused on rewards and outcomes, or parameters meant to make us the best rule-followers, but by affections that move us closer to him.

As we grow in faith, we must not fall into the temptation of seeking spontaneous or immediate results, much less results based on when and how we want them. True growth is not characterized by us, or by what we understand according to the world. The result of sin was deprivation of our relationship with Jesus Christ. But the result of grace is a rejoining of this

---

[4] Herman Bavinck, "The World-Conquering Power of Faith," in John Bolt, *Bavinck on the Christian Life: Following Jesus in Faithful Service* (Wheaton, IL: Crossway, 2015), 239. A sermon on 1 John 5:4b, delivered in the Burgwalkerk, Kampen, June 30, 1901.

relationship; we, in Christ, are in a mystical union wherein we can experience the fullness of new life—results are found in and characterized by him. As we recall from previous chapters, faith is given and increased by our proximity to saving knowledge of our Christ, to grow in faith is to grow in preference for Jesus' lordship in our lives, to be moved in our affections toward him. We cannot determine the results we should expect apart from what he reveals according to Scripture. If we are compelled by the Holy Spirit to know Jesus more, the outcome will be measured against his Word to us.

Faithfully knowing

How do we fight for a right practice in saving faith? Jonathan Edwards once preached, "There can be no love without knowledge. It is not according to the nature of the human soul, to love an object which is entirely unknown. The heart cannot be set upon an object of which there is no idea in the understanding."[5] Are we compelled to some form of affections—even if we aren't sure what it might be right now? As pilgrims, we are called to train our affections to be restricted to saving faith, the knowledge of scriptural truths. We are perpetual learners of how to rightly practice what Christ desires of us, as well as the ways wherein he gifted us.

Saving faith, in practice, is a constant assessment of how we organize our knowledge. We cannot love what we do not know. The more we diminish God in our thoughts, the more we will think less of him, and the less we think of God, the less frequently we will pray to him; the less we pray the further diminished will be our understanding and intimacy with the triune

---

[5] Jonathan Edwards, *On Knowing Christ* (Carlisle, PA: Banner of Truth, 1990), 14-15.

God. Satan cripples our spiritual vigor by such a viciously simple cycle. He does not necessarily cripple Christ's church by our mistakes and moral failures, but by a chilling of affections, increased apathy, and sly stagnancy in discipline. Assessing our affections, and what we do with what we know is essential to getting back on the right growth path for our gift of faith.

Against prideful affection
Now we must acknowledge here that false faith, as described in the previous chapter, will often cause us to think that the work of faith is to speak and believe in the things we want. Many modern false prophets teach us to declare and decree our opinion on our situation in life, as if we have the power of the Creator to work for our own desires. This is a compulsion of faith in ourselves, not compelled by affections for the things of God nor humbled or submissive to Christ as our true Lord. Seeking after our comfort slowly but surely moves us further from a true affection for Christ and isolates us from the body of Christ. Faithless comfort is a twofold emptiness that bolsters our pride while it stifles our joy. Affections for our own welfare place faith in circumstances and in our own covetousness.

Nowhere does Scripture compel us to call on God for our own desires, this is very clearly warned against through the sorcerer Simon Magus (see Acts 8:9-24), who sought to benefit his clout, position, and finances by performing in the name of Jesus. Faith is not a means to obtain our end, but it is a compulsion to see Christ's end—his glory perfectly displayed. Compulsion for Christ's end inevitably leads to humility. We don't exercise faith that God is going to act a certain way, but trust in the nature and attributes of God as we grow to know and recognize him more despite our earthly desires. He is good and trustworthy, merciful, just, and perfectly consistent. The purpose of his giving us the propositions within Scripture is that our new faith-filled eyes would see how to apply his Word (Ps. 119:36). The purpose is never that we obtain all our desires, but that he is glorified and that we enjoy resting in his glory as we come to know it more.

Practicing faith does not look like the egoism of giving and receiving transactions. The Lord is not impressed with us as purveyors of his doctrines, but he is pleased when we are obedient to them. Faith is never dependent upon *our* works or exertions (Rom. 9:16). Even if we described faith as our exertion, we would be burdened to say that he rewards despite what we do. When our affections are rested on what we believe is best for us, or what God can do for us, we are serving an idol made of our limited circumstantial constructs. If the outcome of faith is our personal satisfaction, then the God who gives us faith is doing a very bad job. This would also indicate that all the practices we do and all the actions we take to grow in our faith are determined by our own preference and by our own ability in how to make ourselves happy. This makes God simply a god of convenience; his lordship shifts according to our shifting preferences and perceptions of that which might make or keep us happy. He is master only over our fleeting wants and passions. He who is lord of convenience is not Lord at all. Even if we don't believe the outcome of faith is our happiness but truly to grow in affections for Jesus Christ, we may still fall prey to the cultural perspective that we must prioritize our personal blessings, that our faith provides for our personal outcomes. So then how do we train for right affections?

Killing sin: our first practice

The first work we experience, empowered by the new life in the Spirit, is repentance. This is not only asking forgiveness, but pruning patterns in our lives that lead us into temptation. Repentance, as understood in previous chapters, is the removal of spiritually toxic predilections, a continuous work of saving faith. We are called to be killing sin; often this is called mortification. Scripture even mentions the artillery useful to the task of digging at the heart and fending off the snares of temptation (Eph. 6:16–17; Heb. 4:12). We know "those who belong to Christ Jesus have crucified the flesh with its passions and desires."[6] We have, in a sense, a duality of positive and negative works: things we ought to do, led by the working of the Spirit in obedience, and things we ought not do—the sin and old self that will always, in this life, be drawn and inclined to sinful behaviors, even if those things seem simple and benign (Rom. 7:14–25). Killing sin is partnered with assurance because only by the Spirit can we identify what does not please God. Only by the Spirit can we recognize the conviction and lifestyle-change necessary for godliness. We praise God for mercy in giving repentance while chastening and protecting us from further detriment to our joy and intimacy with him.

We are always to be looking for sin. The Holy Spirit is the magnifying glass that reveals the darkest parts we cannot fathom on our own. Where in my heart, when I truly ruminate on God's Word, do I see sin lurking? This is such a bold question because at its core we understand repentance leads us to see Christ working within us. We need his focused lens to truly direct our eyes to the otherwise hidden sin in our depraved hearts. As John Owen said,

---

[6] Galatians 5:24.

How can I practice my faith?

> When sin lets us alone we may let sin alone; but as sin is never less quiet than when it seems to be most quiet, and its waters are for the most part deep when they are still, so ought our contrivances against it to be vigorous at all times and in all conditions, even where there is least suspicion.[7]

To mortify sin is to see Christ victorious within us, leading us and training us to attack the enemy where we least expect him. By holy remembrance the Spirit teaches us to dig for that which would soon hurt.

Through killing sin we work to rid ourselves of false affections. The best place to be, the ultimate habit to form in the life of one mortifying sin, is to join the body of Christ, the local church. As we read in Hebrews 10:24–25, though no church is perfect yet, this text promises the local body is a place wherein our affections are stirred positively as we sit under the preached Word and among those training in righteousness just like us. We know our worship in the body is not for entertainment or personal inspiration, but corporate glorification of who we corporately adore. Elders and youngsters alike are there practicing at least one means of grace per week (prayer, the Lord's supper, baptism, reading of the Word, and singing of Christ). Being stirred in this place will help us ask, "Am I looking and living like the former saints?" Community helps convict sinners to mortify sin and, just as important, grow saints in greater works of faith. The local church is both a magnifying glass for sin and a salve toward its cure.

---

[7] John Owen, *Overcoming Sin and Temptation*, ed. Kelly M. Kapic and Justin Taylor (Wheaton, IL: Crossway, 2006), 51.

The works of faith

Saving faith teaches God elected some to believe in him for salvation, but he also elected those same persons to be capable of working out sanctification—holy works of obedience born out of affections for the savior (Ezek. 36:27). God spoke of us through Paul in Ephesians 2:10, "For we are his workmanship, created in Christ Jesus for good works, which God prepared beforehand, that we should walk in them." The purpose of faith is to glorify God, and God chose for our faith to be the means of showing his glory through works that please him (Rom. 15:6-7). Charles Spurgeon once wrote,

> Saving faith appropriates the finished work of the Lord Jesus, and so saves by itself alone, for we are justified by faith without works; but the faith which is without works cannot bring salvation to any man. We are saved by faith without works, but not by *a* faith that is without works, for the real faith that saves the soul works by love and purifies the character.[8]

Is our character being transformed? Saving faith pursues not only spiritual formation, but character forming evidences of such faith—our entire lifestyle will shift toward holiness.

The gift of faith is the same as the gift of the Holy Spirit. It is the Spirit's work within us that gives us new sight, new perspective, new passions, new affections. But we are called to the work of experiencing and evidencing such giftedness. We may often see ourselves as not gifted in a particular way or strength, boldness or aptitude, but Satan schemes through the delusion of comparison. Sure, some experience greater sensations of

---

[8] Charles Spurgeon, *The Soul-Winner* (Geanies House, Fearn, Ross-shire, GB: Christian Focus, 2015), 164.

grace than you. Some are better at hospitality, just as some are miserable at fasting. But that does not negate the work and gift of the Holy Spirit. As one man wrote on the this promise of the Spirit, "[Baptism of the Spirit] was not reserved for a more advanced breed of Christians. It applies to all who were or are effectually called into a saving union with the exalted Christ."[9] There is no spectacular performances or specific manifestation that proves faith, but the work of faith is best seen in irrepressible pursuit of the Giver.

Faith and habit
One issue that effects our works of faith is personal habit. As I contemplate faith habits, I realize my failures at follow-through; where I've started reading a particular devotional each morning and then grew lax to the point where that journal or reading hasn't been opened in a year. Is this your experience? I also remember my daughters' wooden blocks. Like those wooden blocks from the good father, he has provided that first row of blocks, our gifted faith, so that, whether we have failed before or not, we may start building again in pursuit of him who is eternally present to his elect. We're after the substance, author, and finisher of our faith—the triune God who sought us and bought us for his glory. His affections are for us as he condescends to help us in our formation heavenward.

We could very easily turn the rest of this chapter into a list of spiritual disciplines.[10] But foundationally, how do spiritual disciplines relate to saving faith? Disciplines are both evidence

---

[9] Walter J. Chantry, *Signs of the Apostles: Observations on Pentecostalism Old and New*, 3rd ed. (Carlisle, PA: Banner of Truth, 1976), 74.

[10] I highly recommend Donald Whitney's *Spiritual Disciplines of the Christian Life* or David Mathis's *Habits of Grace* for a thorough guide in several disciplines and a greater expression of how to practice each of them.

of our right affections for Christ and exercise in experiencing Christ's affections for us. Simultaneous to this discipline is the spiritual fruit of discernment of our union with Christ, joy with him, strength for perseverance, love for his people, and gifts for his church. As we've learned, saving faith is an affectionate knowledge of the scriptural truths revealed to us of Jesus Christ. Those disciplines which lead us to first, grow in knowledge, and second, grow in experience of that knowledge, will necessarily grow our faith. Key to all our practices is a regard that Scripture is sufficient for faith, such that we not only treat Scripture as authoritative, but practice this authority through obedience. Based on Scripture's prescription we are to pray, read and memorize Scripture, commune together in the local body, sing songs, hymns, and spiritual songs, teach and baptize, fast, give of our finances as well as ourselves, and sit under gospel preaching.[11] This is a short list, but it is a determinative list.

In these disciplines we practice saving faith as it leads us to account for our faith within a community under Christ's authority. Unity in the body comes from affections toward a fixed object. Our relationship with confessing church members gives us freedom to confront one another and encourage one another in our shared pursuits. But we practice these things as an outpouring of our affections for his authority, in humility and worship.

The practice of faith is observed most clearly in applying and obeying faith statements. We evidence our faith through these means, by sharing the truths of God's Word with other

---

[11] References for these disciplines include, in order: Ephesians 6:18 & 1 Thessalonians 5:16-18; Joshua 1:8 & Psalm 119:11; 1 Corinthians 12:12-27; Colossians 3:16; Matthew 28:19-20; Matthew 6:16-18; Romans 12:1 & Hebrews 13:16; Romans 10:17.

believers and together conforming our hearts. In a shared spirit of faith, we conform our hearts to the authority of Scripture among those who will willingly challenge our misconceptions of how to apply God's Word. We desperately need rebuke and correction if we seek to grow in both repentance and faith. Since our God-given disciplines are not results-based, reward-driven, or for personal achievement, one necessary scriptural discipline we must accept concerning faith is the role of suffering as a fruit-bearing gift of faith (Phil. 1:29).

Faith and trials
Everything that we have, be it knowledge, color, gender, finances, upbringing, sickness, pleasure, despair, or joy is a gift from God that we must honor as stewards under a master to whom we will give account. Faith calls us to obedience no matter our context or circumstances. Even in the most difficult struggles, the Holy Spirit shepherds us to be wise stewards of our portion in this life. How can we use circumstances to grow in the affections of Jesus Christ? That is the question for practicing faith in the face of suffering. Nothing strange is happening to us when we encounter suffering (1 Pet. 4:12), and certainly nothing is out of God's control (Ps. 139:16). As James 1:2–4 (NASB) reads, "Consider it all joy, my brothers and sisters, when you encounter various trials, knowing that the testing of your faith produces endurance. And let endurance have its perfect result, so that you may be perfect and complete, lacking in nothing." Trials test not only our obedience, but our affections—and do so for our holiness. A well-seasoned affectionate knowledge can still grow weary in trial, but it will not weary completely because Jesus Christ is still Lord. Such weariness will be refined as holiness in patient humility.

Christians who trust the faithfulness of Christ do not seek trials and tribulations, but they are able to welcome them as a discipline for refining godly habits and purging sinful habits, pride, and especially the prideful thought that faith is based on exertion. When we welcome struggle rather than allow it to bring despair, we are practicing perseverance. Perseverance produces fruit; through faith in the Lord's preservation, we are made capable of growing more in trials than we could have expected otherwise (Rom. 5:3-5). We grow by applying the truths we confess, actively professing them through our whole selves. Where Satan would compel us to despair, we have the power to seek after those things we know of Christ and make even our darkest hour rich in grace, mercy, and tested doctrines of God's attributes. The faith of the early church grew and was strengthened during hardship and persecution. Knowing how to preach the gospel in the face of trials, sufferings, and doubt is our greatest discipline for spiritual health and vigor. We are not being formed for earthly satisfaction, but are being shepherded into eternal glory—such glory shines even brighter as we rest in the embrace of our Savior who can turn the darkest night into the brightest haven, a light incomprehensible to the world.

Conclusion

We practice our faith as prescribed, not as we wish. How do we practice our saving faith? We do so as wingless bird, suddenly, unchangeably, supernaturally gifted powerful wings for flight. We are to grow in this gracious power as we come to know our Gifter more and more. This is experienced through applying our knowledge of him through his Word. We examine our affections for him by learning about him—how to be obedient, how to grow with others, and how to form new practices in our day to day life. As our knowledge grows, so must our application; and as our application grows, so will our affections.

Our saving faith is not our product, but it is our responsibility. Our assurance is directly linked to our inclination in forming habits of grace, how we choose to practice and form patterns in our lives that reflect our affections for what God has revealed to us in his authoritative Word. Essential to these habits is that of killing sin. As our affections grow toward Jesus Christ, so must our despair and hatred for sin; if we do not hate sin, we do not love our Savior. As our knowledge of doctrines and the person of Jesus Christ grows, the Spirit will enlighten us to see where we can grow and where we must purge sinful thoughts, attitudes, and actions.

Through these faith-works we lead the lost to recognize a Savior who has established, and continues to establish, his heavenly kingdom here on earth as we long for its fulfillment. Our best practice for growing in saving faith is by sharing it with others as we conform to the kingdom hereafter. So, what does sharing our faith look like and why do share it?

Examining our affections:

1. What are some things you have great affections for? How would you measure or rate your affections for Scripture over or under these other things in your life?
2. What does mortification of sin look like in your life? How are we to stir up others for good works? How do we help others to kill sin without creating further conflict?
3. What are some of your current disciplines for growing in faith? What people in your church experience have had the greatest impact on your personal spiritual disciplines?
4. How does faith in the person of Jesus grow by being obedient, or doing good things? How does the Holy Spirit grow us through obedience?
5. Have you observed the results of a prideful faith? Explain. How might a prideful faith lead others to stray? What are some of the ways we turn our spiritual practices into a means for our own convenience or happiness? How can we fix this?
6. What trials in your life have helped you to grow in your affectionate knowledge of Jesus Christ? Are there trials that have hurt your affections for Jesus? Is there a particular attribute of the person Jesus that you rely on most (a certain trait or quality you seek) when you are suffering?

6
If faith is a gift, then why evangelize?

If faith is gifted by sovereign decree long before anyone is born, then why bother sharing the gospel? This is typically the sentiment associated with the doctrine of election—yes, faith is connected to election, but nowhere in Scripture does election negate evangelism. We began our study with a plane illustration, let's now circle back to our two friends attempting their journey. Saving faith is not climbing over a fence, racing down the tarmac, and hanging onto a wing. When we, who are safely in the plane, look out the window and see that man wrongly attempting to fly, there are two ways we falter in evangelism. The first is to see the man hanging on the wing as some sordid scoundrel who will get what he deserves as the plane takes off. The second is to see this man as a special case who is well-meaning and may certainly get to his destination because everyone has their own path. Both assume a subjective, relativistic faith, but as we've learned there is only one infallible, saving faith and that through Jesus Christ.

We with saving faith are called to be soul-winners—not apathetically watching some person try to hang on the wing of a plane where death is inevitable, but to reach out the window with a free ticket. Surely there is no place in Scripture that calls people to "accept Jesus into their hearts," but there is abundant proof in Scripture that no one comes to belief and repentance without a call and charge from a believer. In Acts 20:24, Paul testified of his gift of saving faith: "I do not account my life of any value nor as precious to myself, if only I may finish my course and the ministry that I received from the Lord Jesus, to testify to the gospel of the grace of God." This is why we *must* also testify to this same gospel.

Word to us

When Paul wrote "I decided to know nothing among you except Jesus Christ and him crucified,"[1] his hearers knew this was true. Their faith was not bound by their experience with Paul, his persuasive arguments, or by their deep personal insights. To be more evangelistic is to grow ever more nurtured and rooted in the doctrines of our Christian faith. True evangelism is not less rooted in doctrine, not compromising, not seeker-friendly—as if we're meeting someone's need for acceptance rather than bringing them to glorify their Creator. The term "evangelism" is rooted in a sharing of faith statements, the gospel, the sound doctrines of Jesus Christ. We are not winning souls by convincing them of rational arguments or hypothetical higher powers; no, we win souls by exposing them to the unrelenting propositions of Scripture whereby God himself meets them. For those in Corinth, and for us today, "faith comes from hearing, and hearing through the word of Christ."[2] Going back to chapter 2 of our study, we know it is the Spirit's work to gift faith. We do not reason unto salvation, earn unto salvation, or feel unto salvation. Scripture alone makes those elect of God *wise* unto salvation. No unregenerate teaching can generate the effects of saving faith; neither can a Christian, by showing off good works in the name of Jesus (without so much as a word of Scripture) call a sinner to the duty of faith.[3]

---

[1] 1 Corinthians 2:2.
[2] Romans 10:17.
[3] Cornelius Van Til, *Christian Apologetics*, 2nd ed. (Phillipsburg, NJ: P&R, 1976, 2003), 94, 104, 131. Van Til's apologetics have come to be called by a very fancy name: revelatory presuppositionalism.

WHY EVANGELIZE?

Without the saving faith produced by God's revealed Word, all that can be known of spiritual knowledge is ambiguous at best. Therefore, we preach Christ, the Word made flesh who makes himself known. Do you recall those Scriptures which first brought to you an affectionate knowledge of Jesus Christ? We diligently examine ourselves; according to the *1689 Baptist Confession*, "it is not providence or creation, but revelation and the promise of the gospel which enable saving faith and repentance."[4] By encountering the word of Christ, the Spirit accomplishes his work according to God's predestination.

Rightly understanding the gift of faith will necessarily shape our evangelism. If it is not by our will or exertion to save ourselves, then it is certainly not in those to whom we witness. If Scripture is the means the Spirit chooses to enliven dead sinners to new life in Christ, then we ought to be diligent in knowing, sharing, and praying Scripture as best and as purely as we can. Revisiting the plane analogy, do we want to lead others to grab hold of the wing based on our choice of music, through our personal stories, our intellect in persuasion, or even socially acceptable half-truths simply to make lukewarm Christianity accessible to someone with whom we're friends? Or do we want them in the cabin, safely harnessed, and able to experience the flight by the stable hand of those leading by way of the propositions of Jesus Christ? We were not led to Christ by irresponsible coercion, and we must not put stock in such methods which distract from the object of faith. The power of evangelism rests in the sovereignty of God; and by his gospel we grab hold of the lost and bring them into the plane.

The reality of Christ's crucifixion and resurrection cannot be deduced through an emotional experience during a praise

---

[4] *The Baptist Confession of Faith 1689*, chapter 20.2.

song, a pithy saying, or a social connection to a church event. Faith is not experience-based; it will not grow on its own as people enjoy the "spiritual" services and interactions we provide. Herman Bavinck leads us to remember,

> Faith is not the ground that carries the truth, nor is it the source from which knowledge flows, it is the soul's organ; it recognizes the objective, self-subsistent truth. Faith is the pail with which the believer draws the water of life from the wellspring of God's Word.[5]

We pour out as much of the wellspring we've absorbed, and we pray. What is supernatural should be confounding. And what is more confounding than evangelism wherein God himself calls and regenerates lost sinners according to his Word working through weak vessels as ourselves? We need not trust ourselves but humble ourselves and trust God's power.

Not mere persuasion
No amount of our own abilities to convince, conjure emotion, or display our intellect will manipulate the Spirit to regenerate a sinner into a saint. We are called to grow wise unto salvation, to grow sound in doctrine, to know our surroundings and practice meditation and application accordingly. We're even called to emote, feel, sense our experiences and the circumstances surrounding us. But these do not necessarily determine our mission for soul-winning. Thomas Aquinas argued, believing based on persuasion or intellect alone is not faith but merit, because we are awarded a measure of faith based on our ability to comprehend or conclude that Jesus' propositions must be

---

[5] Herman Bavinck, *The Certainty of Faith* (St. Catharines, ON: Paideia Press, 1980), 67, 83.

Why evangelize?

true.⁶ Real assent is by divine invitation, not human opinion. And yet, Scripture indeed commands that every soul on earth believe on Jesus Christ; "saving faith is the duty of all," as they hear the gospel and obey.⁷

We're not seeking a decision; we're proving the Spirit. When our evangelism is shaped by the context of the world's depravity, we see how futile it is to seek to give Scripture knowledge and so convince someone unto faith and repentance. *Our* context must be the sovereign grace of faith, no matter the context of those around us. Romans 1:18–23 frames our prayerful consideration of evangelism.⁸ Man cannot reason on the things of God without saving faith. This will cause us to deal with our own need to examine our affections—"Do I know the person Jesus Christ by a supernatural faith?" We do not argue with the lost, but we share the testimony of who Jesus is based on our own sincere affections for him. Removing the blinders of reason, emotion, or persuasion will challenge us to make no assumptions as to when and where the Spirit will move through our evangelism. Our desire is to see his name exalted and his works proclaimed to those who truly need him, and that means every soul we meet (Isa. 12:4). If our affections are sincere, they will be convicting because they are borne of the Spirit and used of God.

---

⁶ Thomas Aquinas, *Nature and Grace: Selections from the Summa Theologica of Thomas Aquinas*, ed. A.M. Fairweather (Louisville: Westminster John Knox, 1954), 257.

⁷ Andrew Fuller, *The Gospel Worthy of All Acceptation* and *The Gospel Its Own Witness*, 2ⁿᵈ ed. (repr; 1801, Ann Arbor, MI: Sovereign Grace Pub., 1961), 23.

⁸ This section of Paul's letter identifies, not only the compulsion we have to create our own wisdom on which others *should* rely, but the depravity of humankind that cannot reason themselves unto God regardless of human knowledge. There is no knowledge of God or God-honoring truth apart from God's revelation, the understanding of which comes singly, thoroughly by faith.

We preach the gospel first. Doctrine must be preached as wholly as the Bible is preached, but evangelism is not based on persuading doctrines but rather on Christ crucified; everyone begins first at the cross. We call folks to the "grammar school of faith and repentance" and as members of our church, we then lead them through "the university of election and predestination."[9] Sound doctrine is essential; but it grows by maturity. Our persuasion of doctrines comes through application, a working understanding in how to take the faith we've been gifted and grow and believe in the world—a living theology. Persuasion does not raise converts, but it grows Christians. It is far sweeter to rejoice with changed hearts, than to boast over challenged minds. So then, how do we win souls without mere persuasion?

Spirit through faith
R.B. Kuiper once wrote "God the Holy Spirit is the author of evangelism"; without the Holy Spirit the church would have destroyed itself in any evangelistic pursuit. "He [the Holy Spirit] calls and leads by divine providence and by his gracious influence on the minds and hearts of those whom he would have sow the seed of the gospel and bring in the harvest."[10] We are indwelt by the Holy Spirit. We were part of harvest chaff, vessels of God's wrath and, under common grace in this lifetime, restrained from being as evil as we possibly could be. We are now vessels of sovereign grace, made for the purpose of pouring out the Spirit's medicine of faith by sharing those same

---

[9] Iain H. Murray, *Spurgeon v. Hyper-Calvinism: The Battle for Gospel Preaching* (Carlisle, PA: Banner of Truth, 2010), 102.
[10] R.B. Kuiper, *God-Centred Evangelism* (Carlisle, PA: Banner of Truth, 2002), 20.

scriptural truths of Jesus Christ which have, by saving faith, stirred our affections to live our lives God-ward.

As vessels of God's sovereign grace, we are to share the truths of Scripture as part of God's effectual calling; this is the means by which the Holy Spirit takes what is received in the lost sinner's mind and causes the heart to hear the truths of Jesus Christ. Chapter 10 of the *1689 Baptist Confession of Faith* examines effectual calling. There we read the Holy Spirit enlivens the elect of God by the Word. By exposure to the doctrines and truths of Scripture "he enlightens their minds spiritually and savingly to understand the things of God." What we see in conversion is not a result of persuasion nor "any power or agency in the creature," be it us or the converted, but the power of the Holy Spirit, "this enabling power is no less than that which raised up Christ from the dead."[11] If this is how God calls the lost, and we have no roster of the Lamb's Book of Life, then it is most clearly our duty to make this call as widely available as humanly possible.

God's infallible, inerrant, authoritative Word is the means the Spirit uses. But let's not downplay the fact that the omnipotent Spirit, he who is the triune God, was working in the time of Paul just as he is working in our churches today. We read in 1 Corinthians 15:3-4, "For I delivered to you as of first importance what I also received: that Christ died for our sins in accordance with the Scriptures, that he was buried, that he was raised on the third day in accordance with the Scriptures." Not only is our message of the gospel in accordance with Scripture, but our calling to proclaim this message as well. The Lord didn't just call Paul, he called us all. We are the Spirit's voice

---

[11] *The Baptist Confession of Faith 1689*, ed. Peter Masters (Oberlin, OH: Wakeman Trust, 1998), 23.

upon the earth as we speak Scripture into the lives of the lost. Richard Longenecker clearly explains, "It is God who brought about the message of the gospel through the person and work of his son, Jesus Christ. But it is also God who, by his Spirit, brings that message to the consciousness of every individual."[12] And through what other vehicle does such power move, but in the preaching, teaching, and ministering of God's own saints—truly by grace we are saved.

We are the outward call

Cornelius Van Til rightly claimed, "God's people must bear witness of God. They have not chosen the task. They have been chosen for it."[13] The church in general, and each of us Christians specifically, are the means for accomplishing the work of effectual calling. We are part of his kingdom come, as indwelled sinners, as vessels made for magnifying Christ. R.C. Sproul writes, "We see the outward call of God in the preaching of the gospel. Everyone who hears the gospel preached is called or summoned to Christ. But not everyone responds positively to this outward call."[14] The external call is the hearing of the gospel; it is absolutely necessary to salvation that the gospel call is heard. However, there is also an internal calling that takes place when the gospel is received by the gifting of faith. By faith we hear the external call and receive it inwardly.

There are two simultaneous calls happening: the outward call to all who hear and the effectual call which is the

---

[12] Richard N. Longenecker, *The Epistle to the Romans*, NIGTC (Grand Rapids, MI: Wm. B. Eerdmans, 2016), 165.

[13] Cornelius Van Til, *Common Grace and the Gospel*, ed. K. Scott Oliphint, 2nd ed. (Phillipsburg, NJ: P&R, 2015), 145.

[14] R.C. Sproul, *What is Reformed Theology?: Understanding the Basics* (Grand Rapids, MI: Baker, 1997, 2016), 168.

outworking of election. The instrument is always the Word of God, not the persuasive intellect of the theologian, not the energy of a charismatic wordsmith, not the guilt of grandma, but the gospel preached, taught, read, or prayed.[15] If we're calling Scripture the instrument, we are the musicians appointed to play the compositions of God through our own fitness and finesse—to play his scales and rejoice in harmony as his church. No matter our profession, education, position in the religious or secular world, we all share in the work of evangelism. As diligent as we are in this work, God has chosen our education, position, and profession in his providence, that we would give excellence in what we do so as to win as many as we can. The message of faith must be richly applied to our everyday lives, so that those whom God appointed for the day of salvation would come in contact with his church even outside the church building. As many as are ordained to eternal life will know the gospel preached through the harmony of the church, even at work (Acts 13:48).

Not just facts
Evangelism is to preach the gospel with the purpose of application, not merely presenting faith as a concept but sharing our saving faith with direct application to sinners. We, as Christians, ought to know Scripture well enough that it shapes our lives. Until Scripture is worth interrupting our daily habits, it will not be worth it for us to interrupt a stranger's, let alone a close friend's life. Therefore it is essential that our spiritual

---

[15] Samuel E. Waldron, *A Modern Exposition of the 1689 Baptist Confession of Faith*, 5th ed. (Wyoming, MI: Evangelical Press, 2016), 179. Waldron explains the clause in 10.2, God's mercy is shown towards those who are incapable of understanding the word. Elect infants and mentally disabled are graciously regenerated unbeknownst to the expectations of the visible church (175-176).

knowledge take deep root. Our doctrine must be practical and then our duties will soon be all the more evangelical.[16] As our knowledge grows so should our affections for applying deeper truths. These fruitful affections are best seen, not in our intentions or wishes, but in how we apply Scripture to those around us—not merely as facts, but as real life-altering doctrines, which we are truly passionate about.[17]

We engage those around us by our own life-altering convictions as we grow in our faith. Too often, the world hears Christians complain about trial as if they had no faith. But what if we believe God is faithful in our trials? The lost would look to us in their turmoil and see truth applied. What if we prioritized worship—testifying to the significance of sitting under God's preached Word? Imagine a world where Christians exposed the prominence and expectations of biblical spirituality—that is a lifestyle that makes it difficult to tune-out propositions of Jesus Christ. Evangelism is a whole lifestyle birthed out of that grand deposit of faith. Not only are we called to evangelism, but the work of evangelism convicts us to analyze our affections.

Many Christians have come to claim Christ based on evangelistic meetings where the expectations of faith were so low that a fleeting emotion is passed off as genuine lifelong affection. Such meetings leave no room for a sinner to count the cost of life-altering scriptural application, for guarding against emotional manipulation, but impose roughshod decision making

---

[16] Nigel Wheeler, *The Pastoral Priorities of 18th Century Baptists: An Examination of Andrew Fuller's Ordination Sermons* (Peterborough, ON: H&E Publishing, 2021), 186. This is from an ordination sermon by Samuel Stennett.

[17] J.I. Packer, *Evangelism and the Sovereignty of God* (Downers Grove, IL: InterVarsity Press, 2008), 44.

Why evangelize?

without deep penetrating thoughtfulness.[18] One may say God saves sinners *despite* this means. Truly, his power is observed in saving a sinner by a single verse. Paul would have much rather rode on the masted sailing vessel than on broken boards all the way to Malta (Acts 27:44). Evangelism is not simply checking boxes, but our own conviction that weighs the whole of eternity upon those to whom we minister. We desire our soul-winning to be the means to get sinners into the safe airplane, not simply smiling and nodding at them as they flap about outside gripping the wing.

Verses for all costs
The Spirit works for God's glory, not our ingenuity. Yet we are to be excellent and vigilant in calling others to the truths of Scripture. John Colquhoun beautifully describes how the Spirit works through our outward call: "The Holy Spirit enables [the lost one] to see and believe that the offer is addressed as particularly to him as if it were directed to him alone, and that God speaks as particularly in it to him as if he spoke to him only."[19] Evangelism isn't a memorized tract, but the whole counsel of God, as it is saturating us either through expository preaching or a daily devotion. Saving faith is distinguished in a regenerate person as evidenced by a desire and submission for "the whole testimony of God."[20] The triune God can use a sermon text on the Trinity to give the gift of faith the same as he might use the parable of the lost sheep.[21] No matter what verse is preached or

---

[18] Packer, *Evangelism*, 83-84.
[19] John Colquhoun, *Saving Faith*, ed. Don Kistler (Orlando, FL: Northampton Press, 2008), 141-142.
[20] Louis Berkhof, *Systematic Theology* (Carlisle, PA: Banner of Truth, 2021), 523.
[21] Gordon H. Clark, *Faith and Saving Faith*, 2nd ed. (Jefferson, MD: Trinity Foundation, 1990), 110.

discussed—be it on a talking donkey, a poorly illustrated teaching on tithing, a walk through 1 Chronicles 1-9—if God's Word is being spoken, the Holy Spirit may choose that very verse to convict a sinner unto faith and repentance. A single verse may bring eternity with Jesus Christ to one lost soul, just as it may grow a disciple in a way no other verse could in such manner. The blessings of God are observed most splendidly when we stop imposing human bias on the Spirit's supernatural work. The same is true for our family worship practice; God equips us to be prepared to call others no matter the station or situation, including those in our household.

Parents to children

Our greatest charge, and a means for growth in saving faith, is household evangelism. Parents are called to teach the Word to our children (Deut. 6:4ff), to remember the works of the Lord in Scripture as well as in the doctrines we have come to understand in our own life (Ps. 145:4; Eph. 6:4; 1 Tim. 4:10-11). We must not assume that our children will become Christians at church or that they're prepared enough without our help. Cornelius Van Til painted an excellent picture when he described a family sending their child into the world without doctrinal knowledge, exclaiming it is "as naïve as jumping off the Empire State building with prayers for a safe landing."[22] The first church our children need is our home, consecrated to biblical parenting. From infancy until they leave the nest, the exposure our children receive in a home dedicated to the Lord is sufficient to salvation, but only so far as the home is scripturally saturated (2 Tim. 3:15). We must not rely on anyone else to

---

[22] John R. Muether, *Cornelius Van Til: Reformed Apologist and Churchman* (Phillipsburg, NJ: P&R, 2008), 81.

assume the task commissioned to us, to raise our children in the Lord. We must not assume anything of our children based on rote memory, desire for baptism, or recitation of catechism questions. This does show that we are doing our duty, but it does not necessarily reveal saving faith. We must not be too quick in trusting particular outward signs or methods, but remember that even if our children are truly confessing saving faith's outward fruit of repentance and affection, the gospel call remains for parents to pour into the spiritual lives of their children. Of course, our desire is for our children to know the Lord with affectionate knowledge; thus we ourselves continue growing in such knowledge, and must continue sharing and evangelizing our children. Even when they come to faith in Jesus, the need for evangelism merely gives way to the need for sanctification within the household! Evangelism isn't only for those outside the church—it is the gospel for all, even those who believe. If the gospel is in the house, it will pour out into the streets. Revelation 7:9 does not work apart from Deuteronomy 6:7.[23]

Conclusion

The love of God and love toward neighbor are the fruit of our affections (Mark 12:30-31). We cannot experience the affections wrought by saving faith apart from a supernatural desire to see others join us in repentance. You may recall our quote

---

[23] Revelation 7:9-10, "After this I looked, and behold, a great multitude that no one could number, from every nation, from all tribes and peoples and languages, standing before the throne and before the Lamb, clothed in white robes, with palm branches in their hands, and crying out with a loud voice, "Salvation belongs to our God who sits on the throne, and to the Lamb.""
Deuteronomy 6:7, "You shall teach them diligently to your children, and shall talk of them when you sit in your house, and when you walk by the way, and when you lie down, and when you rise."

from Andrew Fuller in the first chapter.[24] By union with Christ in salvation, we will share his heart; that means we will share a compulsion to see sinners saved, our affections will be not only for Christ but will match his desire and will. Knowing the doctrine of God's sovereign decree in salvation gives assurance that when we, as blessed means toward his glorious end, preach or teach Christ he is using us. He thought of the conversation before time began. He chose it to be the catalyst that brought a sinner before the cross. In evangelism, we are recognizing our presence in God's eternal will, and one day we will see his fruit ripened in heaven. Are we living in his will, believing he really saves sinners through the means of his feeble, but faithful people? He has. He does. He will.

Fanny Crosby has a wonderful verse on evangelism.

> Rescue the perishing, care for the dying,
> Snatch them in pity from sin and the grave
> Weep o'er the erring one, lift up the fallen,
> Tell them of Jesus the mighty to save
>
> Rescue the perishing, duty demands it;
> Strength for thy labor the Lord will provide;
> Back to the narrow way patiently win them,
> Tell the poor wanderer a Savior has died.[25]
>
> Rescue the perishing, care for the dying,
> Jesus is merciful, Jesus will save.

---

[24] See page 7 of this volume. Andrew Fuller, *Strictures on Sandemanianism in Twelve Letters to a Friend* (New York: Richard Scott, 1812), 152.

[25] "Rescue the Perishing," in *Eternal Praise: For the Church and Sunday School*, ed. Marion Lawrance and E.O. Excell (Chicago, IL: Hope Publishing Co., 1917), 320.

Let all the pressure and expectation be upon him who gifts faith and regenerates the dead to life, but let us be the means to do all he commands for calling and loving those who are perishing yet in sin. Our duty, if we trust not only our assurance but our purpose in faith, is to glorify Christ as Savior and Lord. Our purpose is to call sinners to repentance as Jesus did (Mark 1:15). The marvelous conclusion of the gospel story if fast approaching—the plane is taxiing to the runway. Do not let another soul pass by without giving them the true gospel ticket for saving faith. Do not let your church, your loved ones, much less the stranger on the metaphorical tarmac, believe that the wing could ever be better than the truly saving seat secured in Christ our Lord.

What is saving faith?

Examining our affections:

1. How did you learn the message of salvation? As you reflect, how has God's power worked through your conversion experience? Who was involved?
2. When were you taught about your role in evangelism? What has been your understanding of the role a person is to take in evangelism?
3. Why might saving faith be the antidote to our fears and neglect of seeking to save souls? How do you connect the doctrine of saving faith with the importance of evangelism? Do you believe a person can have some knowledge of truth, theology, religion without being regenerate?
4. Who have you most recently shared the message of the gospel with? What Scripture have you used in the past? Why might we believe some Scripture is more important than others in evangelism? Explain how this could be good or bad.
5. How might persuasive or experience-based tactics in evangelism lead to a weakening of biblical knowledge in the church? How might we reconcile programs designed for attracting people with what we understand as a biblical saving faith?
6. Why is the parents' role in the spirituality of their children such an important aspect of Christian teaching in evangelism? How are we to see this role take shape in our church?

Conclusion

Paul responds to his fellow churchmen in 1 Corinthians 2:2, "For I determined to know nothing among you except Jesus Christ, and him crucified." Paul's language for the word *know* is important; he judged that it was worthless to *consider*, to *appreciate*, to *flood his thinking* with anything except that which was most important to both him and his hearers—the gospel. The knowing to which Paul refers is affectionate knowledge, the knowledge of the object of our faith. Paul determined to clear his head, to make it so that his complete, whole person was a walking tract of faith statements, propositions that others might cling to by the work of the Holy Spirit. Paul was a walking "confession of hope" (Heb. 10:23). That is the Christian ideal.

Sherlock Holmes, in *A Study in Scarlet*, regards the mystery of expert deduction with a simple illustration as to how he so disciplined his mind:

> I consider that a man's brain originally is like a little empty attic, and you have to stock it with such furniture as you choose. A fool takes in all the lumber of every sort that he comes across, so that the knowledge which might be useful to him gets crowded out, or at best is jumbled up with a lot of other things.... Now the skillful workman is very careful indeed as to what he takes into his brain-attic. He will have nothing but the tools which may help

him in doing his work, but of these he has a large assortment and all in the most perfect order.[1]

This is the picture of a trained, rewired brain. We are called to train our affections, our hearts, the throne within us. Saving faith is an affectionate knowledge of Jesus Christ, according to his Word. This faith is meant to grow and increase as we desire him more and more no matter the circumstances of this life. Perpetually, we are storing up in our "brain-attic" the things of God, filling our minds as our minds pours into our heart. We are to be cautious and discerning about what winds up in our hearts and whatever seeks to draw our affections away from Christ, because that throne within us will be occupied one day forever. Are we careful "workmen"? Are we actively growing more focused and centralized on the prize of Jesus Christ? If there is struggle in that direction, which there is everyday for most Christians I know (namely myself), then we must remember to go back to the Word and draw ourselves closer to the doctrines presented therein.

We are called to be able to meditate on Christ and his doctrines to defeat schemes of Satan (2 Chr. 20:15; 1 Pet. 5:8-9). In Christ, we are able to assess all the circumstances, philosophies, and worldly wisdom that inundates us, as we meditate on the truths of Scripture and grow by making such thoughts obedient to Christ (2 Cor. 10:5). We are to be wise as serpents and innocent as doves (Matt. 10:16). We are to be wise stewards of a working mind, and blessed receivers of a faithful heart. We are to be praying the Spirit applies the truths of God's Word that we might grow more affectionate as the Day of Hope

---

[1] Arthur Conan Doyle, "A Study in Scarlet," in *The Annotated Sherlock Holmes*, vol. 1, ed. William S. Baring-Gould (New York: Clarkson N. Potter, 1967), 154.

Conclusion

draws nearer; prudent and diligent in the faith delivered to us as we first heard it preached and taught (Deut. 13:14; Rom. 10:14).

Saving faith is an essential doctrine in the church. There are multitudes of Christians engaged in churches that have not stressed the importance of grounded, biblically defined faith. This is to the detriment and anxiety of those whom God has called. It is not just the duty of pastors, but of fellow church-members and saints, to rise to the occasion, to teach doctrine with urgency. If the Spirit has enlivened you, your faith is assured. Your life is new. You are saved.

With saving faith comes all the graces of repentance, spiritual growth, assurance, and supernatural union with Christ and his church. Just as important, with saving faith comes the promise that this union is leading us somewhere, and we are gifted a conviction of that somewhere (Heb. 11:1). Our faith will one day be made sight—the mystery will be revealed, not just in truth but before our very eyes. Though we see only dimly, through the staggering fog of our present life, in the twinkling of faith-beheld eyes, one day we shall know our Lord fully and completely (1 Cor. 13:12). Our spiritual growth, our repentance, and all other graces will come to a spectacular, glorious fruition on the same day we see Christ Jesus. And only saving faith is that faith which *will* be fulfilled—when we "*will* see his face" (Rev. 22:4).

I write this book for that eighteen-year-old boy coming up out of the water, wondering—misguidedly—if this was just an act, if God really wanted me, if I was going to mess it all up. I pray this book will help you to know a bit more about the journey of faith that begins with a loving Father, and not with you (so you can't mess it up).

Excursus:
On *saving faith* and the biblical language of amounts

If faith is a gift, why does Jesus talk to his disciples as those with "little faith" (Matt. 17:20)? Did they not obtain a required measure? Or did God not provide as adequately as he should have? This question is important because of what we know even in our present church experiences. There are figures who contend that they have been gifted a unique, miracle-producing faith, and there are those who have had faith visions, or those who have assumedly obtained a powerful kind of faith to dish out blessings based on financial transaction. None of these circumstances come from a scriptural interpretation of faith. You are not less of a Christian for lacking in their experiences. So, then what do we make of the biblical language of *amounts* of faith?

If saving faith is an affectionate knowledge of Scriptural truths concerning Jesus Christ, then we do indeed grow in our faith—however, not as some might think. The abovementioned verse does not refer to a diminutive quality of the disciples' gifted faith; their faith has saved them wholly, with life-altering trust and dependence. This diminutive language refers to their quantity of propositions concerning the one on whom they place affections, the one who saves, the giver of faith. The object of faith remains the same (Heb. 13:8; Rev. 13:8), but the degree to which they understood was limited at this point, therefore their tendency was to underemphasize Jesus' nature and attributes. Jesus charges those who have affections for him to grow in the propositions, perceptions, and knowledge so that their affections will be of far greater outward expression and holiness. This is how we understand the language of *amounts* of faith, not that one disciple is at time more or less saved than another. Let's observe some instances of this language.

Mustard seed
In Matthew 17:20, Jesus says that faith the size of a mustard seed can move mountains. This is not Jesus seeking for his people to point their affections toward their own abilities, their power and prestige in having such impressive faith. Jesus is indicating that the disciples have yet to comprehend the almighty attributes of their Savior. He, the object of their faith, could easily move mountains, after all, he created earth by his very breath. We ought to pray to him accordingly! The mustard seed analogy is meant to prod the disciples to ask greater things as they place greater affections in the one to whom they pray. The analogy strikes at the exercise and outward expression of the disciples' (and our own) saving faith. When God gifted us with saving faith, he did not give a useless amount. Even while some early believers received extraordinary confidence while the Scriptures were yet complete (1 Cor. 12:9), this certainty they experienced is not the same as the saving faith gifted to God's flock.[1] He did not forget something. He did not expect us to add human power to it. Jesus is the author and finisher, the perfecter of our faith. The expectation is for us to ground

---

[1] D.A. Carson, *Showing the Spirit: A Theological Exposition of 1 Corinthians 12-14* (Grand Rapids, MI: Baker, 1992), 38-39. For the futility in seeking after these specific pre-New Testament gifts see Walter J. Chantry, *Signs of the Apostles: Observations on Pentecostalism Old and New*, 3rd ed. (1976; repr., Carlisle, PA: Banner of Truth, 2018), 33-51.

our faith in the truth of who Jesus is. Are we expressing our faith in him in such a way that adequately depicts or enlivens us to the full, immeasurable glory of Jesus Christ?

"Little faith" dialogue appears in much the same way in the account of Jesus and Peter upon the Sea of Galilee. The specific phrase appears in Matthew 14:22-33; here Peter, convinced of the propositions of Jesus Christ, asks to join his Lord walking upon the stormy waves. He steps out of the boat at his master's command, with eyes fixed upon Jesus, acknowledging, trusting, convinced of who Jesus is—living out affections singly toward the Lord and Savior of the universe. But then he begins to draw upon his worldly affections, giving glory to the storm and those treacherous waters. He diminishes his desire to live out affections for Christ and instead raises affections for the world—his own doubts. Jesus, after Peter finally calls for his Lord, reaches and saves the disciple from drowning. In verse 31, Jesus chastens him, "you of little faith!" But then the Lord asks him a question that strikes at the heart of saving faith and our present language conundrum; "for what purpose"[2] would you place affections in anything other than your Lord and Savior? Is it worth it to trust the things of the world, circumstances, challenges, emotions, fantastic experiences over and against the one who will save you for eternity? Little faith is that kind which places priority in all that serves to distract from the object of faith. The object of our faith is not small, but our affections for him must grow, and our perception of Christ in glory ought to be trained, habitual, impenetrable. We place our hearts upon Jesus Christ steadfastly, though we are little and our faith is frail. The strength of our faith, our hearts, our

---

[2] Charles L. Quarles, *Matthew*, Exegetical Guide to the Greek New Testament (Nashville, TN: B&H Publishing, 2017), 167.

affections does not rest on us, but upon him who is unperturbed in his affections for us, though the wind and waves would drown our little hearts.

"Your faith has… "
Our framework, that little faith refers to a diminished perception of the object of faith, has implications for the *amount of faith* language in several healing accounts as well. The woman with the blood issue has a faith of particular note (Luke 8:48), but she is not alone in this regard. We do not have a blind faith, but one that reasons, has an object, and communicates order and peace of the one to whom we attribute the gift of faith. Saving faith is not only received in an orderly manner, but in a manner that is consistent and makes sense to the recipient. As the Lord speaks, "all things must be done in a properly and in an orderly manner,"[3] including both receiving and growing in faith. For us this means faith corresponds to knowing and growing in the doctrines and attributes of the one to whom we praise. As we read the examples of healing and transformation, we understand faith is a gift of spiritual healing; but how do we process a faith that occasionally heals physically or psychologically?

Let's look to the events of those whom faith made well. Our framework in this volume helps interpret the New Testament phrases, "Your faith has … made you well, made you whole, healed you, or saved you."[4] The recipients of this transformation did not receive or exercise a *certain amount* of faith which led to the healing. There was no transaction or

---

[3] 1 Corinthians 14:40.
[4] This sentence draws from at least the following accounts in the gospels: Matthew 9:22; Mark 5:34; 10:52; Luke 7:50; 8:48; 17:19; 18:42.

manipulation that occurred to manifest their transformation. However, through these miracles the Lord revealed himself to individuals and affirmed the veracity of what they knew of him. Faith is not a promise of perfect physical wholeness, but physical healing at times affirms the future glory of Jesus Christ. Just as we do not reduce faith to a temporary feeling or emotional experience, so we must not reduce it to a physical benefit or financial opportunity. Our faith is nourished by Christ's faithfulness and not our personal experiences. In the background of these miracles it is as if Jesus is saying, "I, the one in whom you have trusted and to whom you have affectionately humbled yourself, have made you well." The regenerate heart of the individual was able to discern the substance of their faith as Jesus Christ gave them a foretaste of his glory. He is showing these witnesses that they now possess the grace and mercy of the object of their faith. We see this vividly in the man who is brought to repentance and saving knowledge, and afterward proven to be inwardly regenerated by having his body regenerated ... that is, healed (Matt. 9:6).

When faith doesn't make well
Interpreting these types of passages without a consistent doctrine of saving faith would hinder the value of sovereign grace. These would not be instances of Christ exercising or exhibiting his holy faithfulness, but rather instances of the grand power of humans who can make whole, make well, heal, or save by act of volition or personal exertion. This is the territory where some folks teach failure, sickness, and suffering are results of not doing, sacrificing, or believing enough (see the example of Job's friends), rather than moments to exercise obedience and thereby commune with Christ even in the darkest, yet still

bountiful circumstances (see Rom. 8:17; Phil. 1:29). At worst, some have interpreted that faith is a neutral mystical power, benign until possessed by a human who has conjured it through personal experience (see Simon Magus). But the miraculous events of Scripture are a confirmation of the reliability, surety, and continuity of the character and promises of God. He not only gifts faith but affirms that the affections of his people are placed rightly in he who makes whole even some on earth, as all his elect will be in heaven.

By faith we hope for heaven; this is a consistent, solid, real hope—as Hebrews 11:1-2 calls it, a "conviction of things not seen." Faith isn't merely trusting a brake pedal *will* work when necessary, it is the car stopped and the pedal touching the floor. We know the truth of our hope with conviction. Such faith is given that we may please the Lord by our trust in his promises. It is never *amounts* of faith, but always growth that concerns Jesus, as we observe in his earthly ministry. Have we grown to trust his promise more today than yesterday? He desires those he gifts to grow in their affectionate knowledge of him, as he, at times, points to the outward expression (through healings) of what is going on in the heart. This is true even of those who are gifted a particularly voracious faith (1 Cor. 12:9), such as those intended to grow, encourage, and lead others in greater affectionate knowledge. These, by providence, know more propositions and applications for obedience (Rom. 16:27) than others, and this for the sake of growth in the body of Christ (Eph. 4:12-13).

Giver of faith

As a final note on this amount language, there is an instance of Jesus speaking to his disciples; in Luke 22:32, where he encourages them with this assurance, "I prayed that your faith wouldn't fail." Surely our faith will never fail (John 10:28), because, as we observe, our faith is stewarded by the triune God (1 Tim. 6:20). Elsewhere, in Luke 17:5, we read of a man praying to Jesus, "Increase my faith!" Jesus is the giver of faith and the grower as well. Our bodies, our families, our finances, our health, our mental state, our car, our job, our friends, our heart—all may fail, but saving faith will not when it is an affectionate knowledge of the scriptural truths of Jesus Christ. We are to increase, discern, and communicate the substance of such faith, but it is not something transacted nor is it manifested by us.

Conclusion

Amounts of faith distinguished in Scripture do not refer to some of us missing out on some of the mystery of the gospel. Such faith does not inform us of powers and prestige. Rather, the language on amounts of faith refers to our affections in the object of our faith and a pursuit toward him. Am I longing to know Jesus as much as I call him my Lord and Savior, or am I disregarding him in my seat of affections? We of little faith are encouraged to dive deeper in pursuit of his spiritual knowledge (1 Cor. 2:5, 12), that we might take such light to a darkened world; that we might bear witness to the only one who can make whole in this life and the eternal life to come. He calls us to pray for greater faith, for spiritual wisdom, and that the work of the Holy Spirit would revive his church to unceasing affections. He does so for his glory as we trustingly point others to the mystery revealed. Lord, increase our faith!

Selected Bibliography

Ames, William. *Marrow of Theology*. Edited by John Dystra Eusden. Grand Rapids, MI: Baker, 1997.

Aquinas, Thomas. *Nature and Grace. Selections from the Summa Theologica of Thomas Aquinas*. Edited by A.M. Fairweather. Louisville, KY: Westminster John Knox, 1954.

Augustine of Hippo. *On the Free Choice of the Will, On Grace and Free Choice, and Other Writings*. Edited by Peter King. New York: Cambridge Press, 2010.

Bavinck, Herman. *The Certainty of Faith*. St. Catharines, ON: Paideia Press, 1980.

Belt, Henk van den. "Herman Bavinck's Lectures on the Certainty of Faith (1891)." *Bavinck Review* 8 (2017): 35–63.

Berkhof, Louis. *Systematic Theology*. Carlisle, PA: Banner of Truth, 2021.

Bolt, John. *Bavinck on the Christian Life: Following Jesus in Faithful Service*. Wheaton, IL: Crossway, 2015.

Brooks, Thomas. *Precious Remedies against Satan's Devices*. Edited by Christopher Ellis Osterbrock.

Peterborough, ON: H&E Publishing, 2020.

Carson, D.A. *Showing the Spirit: A Theological Exposition of 1 Corinthians 12–14*. Grand Rapids, MI: Baker Book House, 1992.

Chantry, Walter J. *Signs of the Apostles: Observations on Pentecostalism Old and New*. 3rd Edition. 1976. Reprint, Carlisle, PA: Banner of Truth, 2018.

Clark, Gordon H. *Faith and Saving Faith*. 2nd Edition. Jefferson, MD: Trinity Foundation, 1990.

Colquhoun, John. *A View of Saving Faith from the Sacred Records*. Edited by Don Kistler. Orlando, FL: Northampton Press, 2008.

Dallimore, Arnold. *George Whitefield*. 2 Volumes. Carlisle, PA: Banner of Truth, 1996.

Doyle, Arthur Conan. *The Annotated Sherlock Holmes: The Four Novels and the Fifty-six Short Stories Complete*. Volume 1. Edited by William S. Baring-Gould. New York: Clarkson N. Potter, 1967.

Dutton, Anne. *Selected Spiritual Writings of Anne Dutton: Eighteenth Century, British-Baptist, Woman Theologian*. Edited by Joann Ford Watson. Macon, GA: Mercer, 2004.

Edwards, Jonathan. *On Knowing Christ*. Carlisle, PA: Banner of Truth, 1990.

Edwards, Jonathan. *On Revival*. Carlisle, PA: Banner of Truth, 1995.

Edwards, Jonathan. *The Religious Affections*. Carlisle, PA: Banner of Truth, 2007.

Eternal Praise: For the Church and Sunday School. Edited by Marion Lawrance and E.O. Excell. Chicago, IL: Hope Publishing Co., 1917.

Fuller, Andrew. *The Gospel Worthy of All Acceptation* and *The Gospel Its Own Witness*. 2nd Edition. 1801. Reprint, Ann Arbor, MI: Sovereign Grace Publishers, 1961.

Fuller, Andrew. *Strictures on Sandemanianism in Twelve Letters to a Friend*. New York: Richard Scott, 1812.

Hodge, Charles. *Systematic Theology*. 3 Volumes. Peabody, MA: Hendrickson, 2016.

Hunter, Robert. *The Complete Annotated Grateful Dead Lyrics: The Collected Lyrics of Robert Hunter and John Barlow, Lyrics to All Original Songs, with Selected Traditional and Cover Songs*. Edited by David Dodd and Alan Trist. New York: Simon & Schuster, 2015.

Kuiper, R.B. *God-centred Evangelism*. Carlisle, PA: Banner of Truth, 2002.

Longenecker, Richard N. *The Epistle to the Romans: A Commentary on the Creek Text*. New International Greek Testament Commentary. Grand Rapids, MI: Wm. B. Eerdmans Publishing Co., 2016.

MacArthur, John. *Saved Without a Doubt: Being Sure of Your Salvation*. 2nd Edition. Colorado Springs, CO: Victor, 2006.

Machen, J. Gresham. *What is Faith?* Grand Rapids, MI: Wm. B. Eerdmans Publishing Co., 1965.

Manton, Thomas. *By Faith: Sermons on Hebrews 11*. Carlisle, PA: Banner of Truth, 2000.

Merkle, Benjamin L. *Ephesians*. Exegetical Guide to the Greek New Testament. Nashville, TN: B&H Publishing, 2016.

Muenther, John R. *Cornelius Van Til: Reformed Apologist and Churchman*. Phillipsburg, NJ: P&R Publishing, 2008.

Murray, Iain H. *Revival & Revivalism: The Making and Marring of American Evangelicalism 1750-1858*. Carlisle, PA: Banner of Truth, 1994.

Murray, Iain H. *Spurgeon v. Hyper-Calvinism: The Battle for Gospel Preaching*. Carlisle, PA: Banner of Truth, 2010.

Murray, John. *The Epistle to the Romans: The English Text with Introduction, Exposition and Notes*. New International Commentary on the New Testament. Grand Rapids, MI: Wm. B. Eerdmans, 1968.

Oliphint, K. Scott. *The Majesty of Mystery: Celebrating the Glory of an Incomprehensible God*. Bellingham, WA: Lexham Press, 2016.

Oliver, Robert W. *History of the English Calvinistic Baptists, 1771–1892 from John Gill to C.H. Spurgeon*. Carlisle, PA: Banner of Truth, 2006.

Olliffe, Matthew. "Is 'Faith' the 'Gift of God'? Reading Ephesians 2:8–10 with the Ancients." https://au.thegospelcoalition.org/article/is-faith-the-gift-of-god-reading-ephesians-28-10-with-the-ancients/. Published 13 September 2017. Accessed 28 July 2021.

Owen, John. *An Exposition of the Epistle to the Hebrews*. 7 Volumes. *The Works of John Owen*. Edited by W.H. Goold. 1855. Reprint, Carlisle, PA: Banner of Truth, 1991.

Owen, John. *Overcoming Sin and Temptation*. Edited by Kelly M. Kapic and Justin Taylor. Wheaton, IL: Crossway, 2006.

Packer, J.I. *Evangelism and the Sovereignty of God*. Downers Grove, IL: InterVarsity Press, 2008.

Prince, David E. *Preaching the Truth as it is in Jesus: A Reader on Andrew Fuller*. Peterborough, ON: H&E Publishing, 2022.

Schumann, Robert. *Schumann on Music: A Selection from the Writings*. Edited by Henry Pleasants. New York: Dover, 1988.

Sproul, R.C. *What is Reformed Theology? Understanding the Basics*. Grand Rapids, MI: Baker, 1997, 2016.

Spurgeon, Charles H. *The Soul Winner*. Geanies House, Fearn, Ross-shire, GB: Christian Focus, 2015.

Turretin, Francis. *Institutes of Eclenctic Theology*. 3 Volumes. Edited by James T. Dennison, Jr. Translated by George Musgrave Giger. Phillipsburg, NJ: P&R Publishing, 1994.

The 1689 Baptist Confession of Faith in Modern English. Edited by Stan Reeves. Cape Coral, FL: Founders Press, 2012, 2017.

The Baptist Confession of Faith 1689. Edited by Peter Masters. Oberlin, OH: Wakeman Trust, 1998.

The Westminster Confession. Carlisle, PA: Banner of Truth, 2018.

Van Til, Cornelius. *Christian Apologetics*. Edited by William Edgar. Phillipsburg, NJ: P&R Publishing, 2003.

Van Til, Cornelius. *Common Grace and the Gospel*. Edited by K. Scott Oliphint. Phillipsburg, NJ: P&R Publishing, 2015.

Waldron, Samuel E. *A Modern Exposition of the 1689 Baptist Confession of Faith*. 5th Edition. Wyoming, MI: Evangelical Press, 2016.

Ware, Bruce A. *God's Greater Glory: The Exalted God of Scripture and the Christian Faith*. Wheaton, IL: Crossway, 2004.

Wheeler, Nigel. *The Pastoral Priorities of 18th Century Baptists: An Examination of Andrew Fuller's Ordination Sermons*. Peterborough, ON: H&E Publishing, 2021.

White, Thomas Joseph. *The Incarnate Lord: A Thomistic Study in Christology*. Washington, DC: The Catholic University of America Press, 2017.

Acknowledgments

This little volume would not be possible without the encouragement of one of my dearest brothers, Rev. Dr. David B. Smith, who took time reading and discussing the topic with me over so many of our lunches. What idea started as an academic tome has become something useful for laypeople within the church. This work would just as well not be in print without the immense editing capabilities of Cheyenne Haste—you and Matt are a dynamic blessing! Likewise, without the suggestion and friendship of Chance Faulkner none of my personal growth through this study nor its writing would see the light of day. Of course, sincerest appreciation to Nate Pickowicz for providing his adept touch to the foreword.

    A thousand thanks to you, reader, for allowing me the privilege of walking with you through the doctrine of saving faith. May the church be blessed to grow in the knowledge of Jesus Christ, until we attain the fulness of he who loved us first.

Subject Index

Affections, 2, 7, 8, 9, 11, 12, 13, 16, 17, 18, 24, 27, 36, 37, 38, 39, 40, 44, 45, 46, 47, 48, 49, 50, 51, 53, 58, 59, 60, 61, 63, 64, 65, 66, 67, 68, 69, 70, 75, 76, 77, 80, 83, 84, 86, 88, 91, 92, 93, 94, 96, 97, 101
American revivalism, 32
Ames, William, 18
Angels, 43
Aquinas, Thomas, 75, 99
Assent, 2, 18, 19, 33, 36, 75
Assurance, 13, 15, 27, 28, 29, 31, 35, 36, 37, 38, 62, 69, 84, 85, 89, 97
Astrology, 21
Augustine of Hippo, 16, 99
Baptism, 1, 10, 43, 63, 83
Bavinck, Herman, 36, 58, 74, 99
Biblical spirituality, 44, 80
Brooks, Thomas, 22
Bunyan, John, 16
Cerebralism, 48, 49
Children, 82, 83, 86
Church history, 43
Clark, Gordon, 37
Colquhoun, John, 28, 81
Crosby, Fanny, 84
Discernment, 40, 66
Discipleship, 14, 31
Doubt, 10, 11, 28, 29, 30, 68
Dutton, Anne, 46, 47, 100

Edwards, Jonathan, 45, 50, 59
Election, 71, 76, 79
Emotionalism, 45, 46
Emotions, 10
Evangelism, 2, 3, 6, 14, 32, 40, 48, 71, 72, 73, 74, 75, 76, 79, 80, 82, 83, 84, 86
Experimental faith, 48
Faith
 amounts of, 91, 92, 96, 97
 as a gift, 91
 as affectionate knowledge, 14, 15, 18, 30, 48, 66, 88, 91
 as assent of the heart, 18
 assurance of, 27
 blind, 19, 20, 40, 94
 definition, 9
 evidence of, 20, 31, 34
 false, 33, 39, 40, 48, 51, 52, 60
 gift of, 3, 6, 9, 21, 24
 object of, 5, 6, 7, 12, 17, 19, 28, 31, 34, 36, 39, 47, 49, 50, 56, 87, 92, 93, 95, 97
 receiving of, 15, 17, 24
Faithfulness of God, 29
Family worship, 48, 82
Feelings, 1, 10, 49, 51, 53
Finney, Charles, 32
Freemasonry, 21

Fuller, Andrew, 7, 41, 56, 80, 84, 104, 105
Ghosts, 43, 53
Gnosticism, 19, 43
Great Awakening, 50
Healing, 45
Heaven, 43, 53, 84, 96, 107
Hell, 43, 53
Hodge, Charles, 16, 20, 28, 101
Holiness, 11, 22, 28, 55, 64, 67, 92
Holmes, Sherlock, 40, 87
Holy Spirit, 1, 8, 10, 11, 12, 15, 16, 17, 18, 19, 20, 21, 23, 24, 27, 31, 32, 35, 36, 41, 44, 45, 46, 50, 59, 62, 63, 64, 65, 67, 69, 70, 72, 73, 74, 75, 76, 77, 78, 81, 82, 87, 88, 89, 97, 100
Hummel, Johann, 39
Judgment, 43
Justification, 2, 55
Knowledge, 1, 2, 7, 8, 11, 12, 18, 20, 21, 23, 25, 36, 37, 40, 42, 47, 48, 49, 51, 58, 59, 66, 67, 68, 69, 70, 73, 74, 75, 80, 82, 83, 86, 87, 92, 95, 96, 97, 107
Local church, 31, 38, 63
Lord's Supper, 10, 63
MacArthur, John, 34
Machen, J. Gresham, 19
Manton, Thomas, 48
Meditation, 3, 7, 20, 39, 74, 88
Miracles, 12, 46, 95
Necromancy, 43
New Ageism, 21
Numerology, 21

Obedience, 3, 11, 13, 18, 20, 23, 30, 31, 34, 37, 38, 49, 55, 57, 58, 62, 64, 66, 67, 70, 95, 96
Owen, John, 21, 62, 103
Parenting, 83, 86
Perseverance, 23, 66, 68
Philosophy, 19, 32
Prayer, 2, 10, 23, 24, 45, 46, 59, 63, 66, 74, 89, 92, 97
Propositions, 6, 7, 8, 11, 12, 15, 18, 19, 21, 22, 23, 25, 30, 37, 42, 61, 72, 73, 75, 80, 87, 91, 92, 93, 96
Regeneration, 1, 10, 11, 16, 17, 18, 20, 22, 23, 25, 29, 56, 57, 74, 79, 85, 95
Regulative principle, 49
Repentance, 3, 22, 23, 24, 25, 62, 67, 71, 73, 75, 76, 82, 83, 84, 85, 89, 95
Revival, 32, 50
Sanctification, 13, 20, 23, 51, 55, 64, 83
Satan, 10, 31, 40, 43, 60, 64, 68, 88, 99
Schumann, Robert, 39, 52
Scripture, 6, 7, 8, 10, 11, 12, 15, 19, 20, 21, 22, 23, 24, 25, 31, 41, 42, 43, 44, 48, 50, 51, 53, 56, 59, 60, 62, 66, 67, 70, 71, 72, 73, 75, 77, 79, 81, 82, 86, 88, 96, 97, 105, 113
Second London Confession, 10, 17, 73, 77, 79, 104
Self-examination, 30, 39, 40
Spiritism, 43
Spiritual disciplines, 31, 65, 70

Index

Spiritualism, 43, 44
Sproul, R.C., 78
Spurgeon, Charles, 64
Temptation, 11, 58, 62
Total Depravity, 15
Trials, 11, 31, 67, 80
Turretin, Francis, 10

Union with Christ, 1, 7, 21, 24, 34, 44, 51, 66, 84, 89
Van Til, Cornelius, 73, 78, 82, 102
Westminster Larger Catechism, 23, 35
Whitefield, George, 17, 100

Scripture Index

Old Testament

Genesis
  15:6 18
Leviticus
  10:1–2 44
Numbers
  23:19 29
Deuteronomy
  6:4 82
  6:7 83
  7:9 29
  13:14 89
Joshua
  1:8 66
Job
  42:2 11
Psalms
  1:3 52
  51:5 15

119:11 66
119:36 61
139:16 67
145:4 82
Proverbs
  3:6 41
  16:6 23
  24:4 20
Isaiah
  12:4 76
  25:1 29
Jeremiah
  17:7 15
  17:9 40
Ezekiel
  36:27 64
  36:22–36 16

New Testament

Matthew
- 6:16–18 ... 66
- 9:6 ... 95
- 9:22 ... 94
- 10:16 ... 88
- 14:22–33 ... 93
- 17:20 ... 91, 92
- 28:19–20 ... 66

Mark
- 1:15 ... 85
- 4:3–9 ... 18
- 5:34 ... 94
- 9:24 ... 36
- 10:52 ... 94
- 12:30–31 ... 83

Luke
- 2:15 ... 6
- 7:50 ... 94
- 8:15 ... 6
- 8:48 ... 94
- 9:23–24 ... 57
- 17:5 ... 36, 52, 97
- 17:19 ... 94
- 18:42 ... 94
- 22:32 ... 96
- 23:33 ... 12
- 23:39 ... 12
- 23:40–43 ... 12

John
- 1:13 ... 11
- 1:14 ... 19
- 3:3 ... 16
- 3:16–18 ... 5
- 5:1 ... 11
- 6:37 ... 28
- 6:44 ... 28
- 6:39–40 ... 28
- 8:24 ... 6
- 10:26-30 ... 27
- 10:28 ... 9, 97
- 14:17 ... 16
- 14:26 ... 16
- 17:17 ... 20

Acts
- 8:9–24 ... 60
- 9:1–19 ... 25
- 13:48 ... 16, 79
- 20:24 ... 71
- 27:44 ... 81

Romans
- 1:18–23 ... 75
- 3:10–11 ... 15
- 4:3 ... 18
- 5:2 ... 13
- 5:9 ... 11
- 5:3–5 ... 68
- 7:14–25 ... 62
- 8:17 ... 96
- 9:16 ... 6, 61
- 10:14 ... 89
- 10:17 ... 66, 72
- 12:1 ... 66
- 12:2 ... 11
- 14:22–23 ... 58
- 15:6–7 ... 64
- 16:27 ... 96
- 16:25–27 ... 22, 57

1 Corinthians
- 1:9 ... 29
- 1:8–9 ... 11
- 2:2 ... 72, 87
- 2:5 ... 97
- 2:12 ... 97
- 2:3–15 ... 16, 21

Scripture Index

4:6 39
7:25 30
12:9 .... 92, 96
12:12–27 66
13:12 89
14:40 94
15:3–4 77
2 Corinthians
3:15 40
10:5 .... 42, 51, 88
10:15 47
13:5 40
Galatians
5:22 16
5:24 62
Ephesians
1:4 16
1:15–18 8
1:4–6 11
2:8 8
2:10 64
2:8–10 103
2:8–9 8
4:18 15
4:20 .... 20, 41
4:12–13 96
5:11 48
6:18 66
6:16–17 62
Philippians
1:16 47
1:29 .... 18, 67, 96
2:12–13 49
Colossians
2:12 10
3:16 66
3:17 11
1 Thessalonians
5:24 30
5:16–18 66

2 Thessalonians
2:10 17
1 Timothy
4:10–11 82
6:20 .... 15, 97
2 Timothy
1:7 19
1:14 15
3:15 .... 6, 83
4:3 42
Hebrews
3:19 29
4:12 62
4:16 36
10:23 .... 28, 87
10:24–25 63
11:1 89
11:6 1
11:1–2 96
11:1–3 7
12:2 39
13:8 91
13:16 66
James
1:2–4 67
2:19 48
1 Peter
1:23 19
1:22–23 6
4:12 67
5:8–9 88
2 Peter
1:1 15
1 John
4:1 41
4:6 41
5:1 11
5:4 58
2 John
1:9 31

Jude
   1:3 15
Revelation
   7:9 83
   7:9–10 83
   13:8 91
   22:4 89

www.ingramcontent.com/pod-product-compliance
Lightning Source LLC
Chambersburg PA
CBHW070915080526
44589CB00013B/1309